Due diligence, tenure and agricultural investment

A guide to the dual responsibilities of private sector
lawyers advising on the acquisition of land and natural resources

Second edition

Kate Cook, Matrix Chambers
for the Development Law Service, FAO

FOOD AND AGRICULTURE ORGANIZATION OF THE UNITED NATIONS

Rome, 2019

Required citation:
FAO. 2019. *Due diligence, tenure and agricultural investment - A guide on the dual responsibilities of private sector lawyers in advising on the acquisition of land and natural resources.* FAO Legal Guide No. 1. Text by Cook, K. Rome. 76 pp.
Licence: CC BY-NC-SA 3.0 IGO.

First edition: January 2019.

ISSN 2664-1607 [print]
E-ISSN 2664-1615 [online]

ISBN 978-92-5-131478-4
© FAO 2019

CONTENTS

Boxes

EXECUTIVE SUMMARY

In the context of continued commercial pressure on agricultural land globally, this guide examines the role and responsibilities of private sector lawyers when advising their clients on agricultural investments. It discusses how lawyers can prevent and/or address and mitigate adverse human rights impacts on holders of legitimate tenure rights when advising on or conducting their due diligence and risk assessment processes on behalf of their clients.

Key international instruments in the areas of land tenure, agricultural investment and human rights have implications for those advising on agricultural investments, including:

- the Voluntary Guidelines on the Responsible Governance of Tenure of Land, Fisheries and Forests in the Context of National Food Security (VGGT);

- the Principles for the Responsible Investment in Agriculture and Food Systems endorsed by the Committee on World Food Security;

- the OECD/FAO Guidance for Responsible Agricultural Supply Chains (OECD/FAO Guidance);

- the associated international human rights laws which underpin aspects of tenure rights.

Tenure-related human rights standards are also relevant to the United Nations Guiding Principles on Business and Human Rights (UNGP) and the responsibility of businesses to respect human rights, to avoid infringing on the human rights of others and to address adverse human rights impacts.

Both the VGGT and the CFS-RAI are non-legally binding but are to be interpreted and applied consistently with existing national and international legal obligations, including human rights obligations. A breach of the VGGT or CFS-RAI is not in itself a breach of human rights law, but may indicate that a violation of human rights law is occurring because the impacts of the breach lead to a violation of human rights (for example where a failure to recognize customary rights of tenure leads to forced evictions and/ or loss of livelihood).

The corporate responsibility to respect human rights under the UNGP has a dual aspect for lawyers: (1) through its impact on the professional duties of the lawyer (including in-house counsel) towards the investor client and (2) through the impact on the law firm's responsibilities as a business in its own right and in the light of its own corporate social responsibility (CSR) commitments. Lawyers have the professional and ethical responsibilities to avoid and address adverse impacts on human rights arising from their own conduct, and to prevent and mitigate impacts that are directly linked to actions of their business clients.

In the light of this dual responsibility, private sector lawyers advising on agricultural investments need to consider how their professional obligations are affected by the standards laid down in the VGGT and CFS-RAI and associated human rights, considering also guidance issued by the International Bar Association (IBA).

IBA guidance highlights the potential role of lawyers as 'wise counsellors' advising in a proactive and pre-emptive way on potential legal risks and exercising professional leverage. The VGGT provide that professionals who provide services to investors should undertake due diligence to the best of their ability when providing their services, irrespective of whether it is specifically requested.

Businesses are required, under UNGP 15(b), to conduct human rights due diligence. Due diligence is also addressed under the VGGT and CFS-RAI. A combined reading of the UNGP and the VGGT confirms that the human rights impact of investments should be factored into due diligence processes. Law firms will wish to be able to demonstrate that they operate due diligence internally as well as supporting their clients to conduct appropriate due diligence. Due diligence is an ongoing process to enable businesses to 'know and show' that they are addressing their human rights impacts through assessing impacts, taking integrated action in response to identified impacts, and tracking and monitoring, and communicating the company's efforts to address its human rights impacts.

Technical guidance for investors stresses risk assessment and that high risk investments should not be proceeded with (FAO 2016). UNGP 23(c) provides that businesses should treat 'the risk of causing or contributing to gross human rights abuses as a legal compliance issue wherever they operate'. It also refers to the need to address violence directed at environmental and land defenders as a human rights risk in the context of large-scale land acquisition, as reflected in the VGGT and in the recently adopted Escazu Convention. These risks relate to the most serious violations of human rights law and rule of law principles and should be a priority for those advising on agricultural investments.

The requirement for meaningful consultation and participation derives from human rights law and is reflected in human rights jurisprudence and in guidance issued by international bodies. The UNGP Principles for Responsible Contracts (Appendix D) which govern state investor contracts, and IBA guidance, as the 10 UNGP contract principles help guide the integration of human rights risk management into contract negotiations.

Businesses must have in place processes to enable the remediation of any adverse human rights impacts they cause or to which they have contributed (UNGP 15(c)). The VGGT confirm that businesses should provide operational level grievance mechanisms where appropriate, where they have caused or contributed to adverse impacts, thus incorporating the duties laid down in the UNGP.

Local communities impacted by agricultural investment are unlikely to have access to legal and technical advice. Law firms can play a key role in ensuring that grievance mechanisms meet standards of fairness and due process, including by ensuring that communities are independently and legally represented in accordance with their own wishes.

Key recommendations include:

- Law firms should review their internal policies on human rights and the UNGP in order to ensure that these incorporate explicit consideration of the protection of legitimate tenure rights and associated human rights. The review should refer to and be informed by the VGGT, the CFS-RAI and the OECD-FAO Guidance and associated technical guidance;

- In-house counsel should ensure that the business has a policy on due diligence which enables it to meet international standards on the protection of tenure rights in the area of agricultural investment and in particular to avoid and address adverse human rights impacts;

- Law firms should ensure that they advise clients on the implications of the VGGT, CFS-RAI and OECD/FAO Guidance in the context of agricultural investment. Legal advisors should ensure that all legal, reputational and financial risks associated with breach of these international standards are brought to the attention of clients, including in the context of due diligence;

- In relation to the drafting of contracts, lawyers should advise that the key issues should be addressed in line with standards laid down in the VGGT and associated human rights including, early meaningful consultation and participation of those likely to be impacted by the investment, transparency, remediation and grievance procedures;

- Law firms should be vigilant to the need to advise clients on the importance of promoting the protection of environmental and human rights defenders who are involved in actions relating to the client's investments;

- Firms should endeavour to ensure that grievance processes are designed and conducted in accordance with due process and fairness standards, and that any tension between these and their professional duty to the client should be raised with the client.

INTRODUCTION

1. INTRODUCTION

1.1   AIM OF THE GUIDE

Large-scale land investments present risks both to investors and to those with tenure rights and other related interests in the land. Lawyers advising on such transactions have a clear professional responsibility to address these risks with their clients and to ensure that international standards, including international human rights protections, are respected. This may not always be straightforward, in part because land which may appear to be 'empty' or idle is in fact often subject to tenure rights, whether or not these are formally protected under national law. The land may also play a vital role in providing food security for local communities in ways that are complex and require close analysis, including legal analysis by reference to relevant human rights law. These complexities should be addressed at the start of the investment process. A failure to address them can result in serious reputational, operational and ultimately financial risks for the investment company and a significant cost to the communities affected by a change in land use. Those providing legal advice in this context can, and should, play a critical role in alerting clients to these risks and addressing them through the international frameworks for business, human rights and tenure, together with relevant national laws.

In 2009, the United Nations Special Rapporteur on the Right to Food highlighted the range of potential adverse impacts of large-scale land acquisitions on the right to food:

> The human right to food would be violated if people depending on land for their livelihoods, including pastoralists, were cut off from access to land, without suitable alternatives; if local incomes were insufficient to compensate for the price effects resulting from the shift towards the production of food for exports; or if the revenues of local smallholders were to fall following the arrival on domestic markets of cheaply priced food, produced on the more competitive large-scale plantations developed thanks to the arrival of the investor…(HRC, 2009).

The Special Rapporteur also raised concerns as to the potential impacts on the rights of indigenous peoples, including the right of free, prior and informed consent (FPIC)[1] under the UN Declaration of the Rights of Indigenous Peoples (UNDRIP) (HRC, 2009). Subsequently, in 2012, the Special Rapporteur addressed access and tenure issues in the fisheries sector and emphasized the pressing need for States to fully implement the VGGT in this sector (GA, 2012).

In the light of such concerns, the Food and Agriculture Organization (FAO) has highlighted the need to prioritize investment models that can reduce or avoid the large-scale transfer of tenure rights as one element in an overall strategy that safeguards tenure rights, while encouraging investment in inclusive business models (FAO, 2015).

FAO and the IBA share some common objectives, such as the promotion of relevant ethical standards in the context of investment in agriculture. In this context, the Legal Office of FAO and the IBA have collaborated to produce this guide, which advises private sectors lawyers on securing responsible investment in agriculture and respect for legitimate tenure rights and other human rights.

Within this framework, this guide highlights the potential role of private sector lawyers in helping to prevent the adverse impacts of these high risk investments on tenure right holders, in particular when advising on due diligence. The guide examines the implications, for the

---

[1] See Section 3.2.2.

DUE DILIGENCE, TENURE AND AGRICULTURAL INVESTMENT

A guide on the dual responsibilities of private sector lawyers in advising on the acquisition of land and natural resources

work of private sector lawyers advising on agricultural investments, of international standards relating to the protection of tenure rights in the context of such due diligence. The relevant international standards include the Voluntary Guidelines on the Responsible Governance of Tenure of Land, Fisheries and Forests in the Context of National Food Security (VGGT, FAO, 2012) and the Principles for Responsible Investment in Agriculture and Food Systems both endorsed by the Committee on World Food Security (CFS-RAI, FAO, 2014),[2] as well as the international human rights laws which underpin aspects of those instruments and other relevant standards, as indicated. The relationship between tenure rights and human rights is addressed further below, including the extent to which adverse impacts on tenure rights are likely to result in, or be associated with, breaches of human rights.

The guide considers these standards in the wider context of the United Nations Guiding Principles on Business and Human Rights (UNGP, 2011),[3] which address the responsibilities which arise for businesses, including law firms, in connection with international human rights law. The UNGP are referenced in both CFS-RAI and VGGT and provide comprehensive authoritative guidance on human rights due diligence.[4] The UNGP are also referred to in the Guidance for Responsible Agricultural Supply Chains, adopted by OECD and FAO in 2016 and which is specifically aimed at businesses (OECD/FAO Guidance). The OECD/FAO Guidance is a framework based on the VGGT, the CFS-RAI and the UNGP, together with the OECD Guidelines for Multinational Enterprises (2011) as well as other international standards and laws, to help enterprises with their supply chain due diligence.

This guide refers to a number of Governance of Tenure Technical Guides (TGs) published by FAO which address specific issues relating to the application of the VGGT including: gender; agricultural investment, respect for FPIC and the protection of rights to the commons, among other issues. They provide useful guidance on the relationship between tenure rights and human rights, as well as highlighting practical and procedural issues relevant to the governance of tenure and to due diligence, in the context of agricultural investment.

The process of due diligence involves specific actions on which lawyers are likely to advise and/or which may be conducted by lawyers. These include surveys of the relevant regulatory context for the investment, the mapping of potential impacts on stakeholders, the conduct of public consultations and negotiations with affected communities, impact assessments and the drafting of contracts and agreements relating to those transactions.

All these standards are directly relevant to the work of private sector lawyers as they advise business clients on agricultural investments, including those entailing the sale or leasing of land and other natural resources. Of central importance is the responsibility of businesses under UNGP 15(b) to conduct human rights due diligence in order to identify, prevent, mitigate and account for how they address their impacts on human rights.

Due diligence is also addressed under the VGGT and CFS-RAI, both by reference to the protection of human rights, and in relation to the protection of legitimate tenure rights (FAO, 2014). The process of due diligence involves specific actions on which lawyers are likely to advise and/or

---

2 The CFS-RAI were endorsed by the CFS in 2014. The ten principles are based upon the concept that responsible investment 'should respect and not infringe on the human rights of others and address adverse human rights impacts. It should safeguard against dispossession of legitimate tenure rights and environmental damage.' (FAO, 2014, p.10).

3 The UNGP have been described as the 'global authoritative framework' on business and human rights , Council of Europe, Committee of Ministers adopted 'Recommendation on human rights and business' (March 37, 2016) www.coe.int/en/web/human-rights-rule-of-law/-/human-rights-and-busine-1, cited in IBA 2016(a), p.6.

4 The UNGP were endorsed by the United Nations Human Rights Council in 2011 by resolution 17/4.

which may be conducted by lawyers. These include surveys of the relevant regulatory context for the investment, the mapping of potential impacts on stakeholders, the conduct of public consultations and negotiations with affected communities, impact assessments and the drafting of contracts and agreements relating to those transactions. Lawyers are also likely to advise on monitoring and reporting arrangements for investments and to be involved in dispute settlement processes relating to investments, including complaints brought under internal grievance mechanisms (UNGP 29).

The guide considers how standards and responsibilities relating to the protection of tenure rights and associated human rights impact on the professional responsibilities of lawyers in the specific context of conducting due diligence. This has to be considered in the light of the corporate responsibility to respect human rights under the UNGP (sometimes referred to as the 'second pillar').[5] It is important to understand that this responsibility has a dual aspect for lawyers: (1) through its impact on the professional duties of the lawyer (including in-house counsel) towards the investor client: advising clients on the implications of these international standards for investments and related transactions in the context of the due diligence which all these standards require; and (2) through the impact on the law firm's responsibilities as a business in its own right: ensuring that the law firm or entity itself meets its own corporate social responsibility (CSR) commitments and other professional standards, including those promoted by the International Bar Association (IBA) and other professional bodies. In this regard, and in the light of the UNGP, the guide considers the professional and ethical responsibilities that lawyers have to avoid and address adverse impacts on human rights arising from their own conduct as linked to, or contributing to, actions of their business clients. The guide takes into account recent guidance issued by the IBA[6] in this area, as well as some regional professional standards.

1.2   THE CONTEXT: COMMERCIAL PRESSURE ON LAND, VGGT AND CFS-RAI

The adoption of the VGGT and CFS-RAI coincided with increased concerns about the impacts of large-scale land acquisition on the tenure rights of small farmers and others with user rights over the land and resources in question (Cotula, 2017(a)), including fisheries and forests.[7] The context for large-scale land acquisition for the purposes of agricultural investment has been one of increased global demand, which appears to have peaked between around 2008-2012, with resulting pressure on access to land and other natural resources (Cotula and Berger, 2017). This has increased the amount of commercial investment in 'marginal land' not previously subject to commercial agriculture and which may be subject to customary and local land rights.[8] New forms of investment, including public private partnerships (PPPs), are being agreed in the commercial agricultural sector and these have attracted support and criticism, in terms of the impacts on small farmers, for example in relation to whether benefits agreed in contracts are actually delivered (Cotula and Berger, 2017).

---

[5] The corporate responsibility to respect human rights is set out in Section II UNGP, Principles 11-24.

[6] This includes the 2015 Business and Human Rights Guidance for Bar Associations (IBA, 2015) and the 2016 Practical Guide for Business Lawyers on Business and Human Rights (IBA, 2016).

[7] This may be particularly relevant in the context of publicly owned lands, see VGGT para 8.3 (FAO, 2012, p.12) which calls for the recognition and protection of such publicly-owned land, fisheries and forests.

[8] See for example the online database at www.landmatrix.org. The Land Matrix is a land monitoring initiative that produces data on land and investment.

A guide on the dual responsibilities of private sector lawyers in advising on the acquisition of land and natural resources

As explained in the technical guide on agricultural investment published by FAO:

> In many developing countries, it can be difficult to identify even formal rights because of weak land administration systems. Land cadastres or registries may be incomplete or non-existent. It can be far more difficult to identify customary rights. As a result, land based investments often fail to take local land rights into account adequately (FAO, 2016).

This has given rise to concern that land transactions related to commercial agribusiness, including long-term leases and concessions, are leading in some cases to the dispossession of poor and marginalised groups, including subsistence or small-scale producers and farmers, pastoralists and other holders of customary rights to natural resources such as rights to graze and forage (Cotula, 2016).[9] In addition to concerns about dispossession and forced evictions, there is also evidence of related adverse impacts on food security and livelihoods, all of which have serious implications for the human rights of those concerned and for the wider communities to which they belong, with consequential legal and reputational risks for investors.

In 2011, a number of CSOs, social movements and international agencies, meeting under the auspices of the International Land Coalition (ILC), issued the Tirana Declaration which calls on all actors to 'actively promote pro-poor, people-centred and environmentally sustainable governance of land and other natural resources' (ILC, 2011). The Declaration denounced all forms of 'land grabbing', defined as acquisitions or concessions that meet one or more of five criteria which include: that they have occurred in violation of human rights; are not based on the FPIC of the affected land-users; or are not based on a thorough assessment, or are in disregard of social, economic and environmental impacts; are not based on transparent contracts that specify clear and binding commitments, or are not based on independent oversight and meaningful participation (ILC, 2011).

The link between human rights and land based investment is also made in the African Union's (AU) Guiding Principles on Large Scale Land Based Investments in Africa (AU Guiding Principles on LSLBI).[10] Fundamental Principle 1 provides that LSLBI respect the human rights of communities, contribute to the responsible governance of land and land-based resources, including respecting customary land rights, and are conducted in compliance with the rule of law.[11]

The extent to which human rights mechanisms and other bodies have characterized these trends as breaches, or potential breaches, of human rights standards serves to underline the ethical, legal and reputational risks and sensitivities associated with investment in this sector where this involves large-scale acquisition of land or rights over land.

Particular concerns have been raised as to the gendered impacts of investments and land transactions on women. These prompted the adoption of General Recommendation No. 34 by the UN Committee on the Elimination of Discrimination against Women (CEDAW, 2016) which addresses discrimination against rural women including in relation to land rights.[12] The VGGT

---

[9] See also FAO, 2015 pages 4-5 and references therein. See also the critical discussion of methodologies in this area in Borras et (2016, p. 12-14), who note the alternative approach used in the database established by the NGO GRAIN.

[10] The 2014 LSLBI General Principles were endorsed by the tripartite consortium of the AU, the UN's Economic Commission for Africa and the African Development Bank in 2014, see https://www.uneca.org/publications/guiding-principles-large-scale-land-based-investments-africa.

[11] See also the Framework and Guidelines (F&G) on Land Policy in Africa endorsed in 2009 by African Heads of States through the Declaration on Land Issues and Challenges. Its implementation is done in recognition of the contribution of the VGGT as another tool to improve land governance on the continent, https://www.uneca.org/publications/framework-and-guidelines-landpolicy-africa - "The Framework and Guidelines on Land Policy is a joint product of the partnership and collaborative effort of the African Union Commission (AUC), the UN Economic Commission for Africa (ECA) and the African Development Bank (AfDB)".

[12] Section G(2)(c) calls on states to ensure that land acquisitions, including land lease contracts, do not violate the rights of rural women or result in forced eviction, and protect them from the negative impacts of acquisition of land by national and transnational companies (CEDAW, 2011, p.18).

directly address gender and the rights of women as do the CFS-RAI (Principle 3 in particular) (FAO, 2015). The UN Committee on Economic, Social and Cultural Rights (CESCR) has highlighted the particular vulnerability of women in the context of forced evictions (CESCR, 1997). Within the UN System, FAO has also promoted the gender equitable governance of tenure (FAO, 2013). The importance of tackling the impacts on women of large-scale agricultural investment is also addressed in the AU's 2014 Guiding Principles on LSLBI. Fundamental Principle 4 calls on LSLBI to respect the land rights of women. The AU has also adopted a Women and Land Initiative.[13]

The VGGT set out a range of measures and safeguards which should be taken by States and non-State actors, including businesses, in the context of transfers and other changes to tenure rights and duties. Paragraph 11.2 provides that States should take measures: 'to prevent undesirable impacts on local communities, indigenous peoples and vulnerable groups that may arise from, inter alia, land speculation, land concentration and abuse of customary forms of tenure'. Investors and their advisors are also addressed directly in the VGGT as having the responsibility to respect national law and legislation:

> ...and recognize and respect tenure rights of others and the rule of law in line with the general principle for non-state actors as contained in these Guidelines. Investments should not contribute to food insecurity and environmental degradation...Professionals who provide services to States, investors and holders of tenure rights to land, fisheries and forests should undertake due diligence to the best of their ability when providing their services, *irrespective of whether it is specifically requested*. (VGGT) (emphasis added).

It is clear therefore that legal advisors, as professional advisors, have a specific and discrete duty to conduct due diligence when providing legal services, taking into account their professional responsibilities. This is consistent with the dual responsibility of law firms as examined in Section 2. In relation to the responsibility to undertake due diligence, whether specifically requested or not, this is an important 'proactive' aspect of the requirement for diligence and is considered further in Section 3.

The particular vulnerability of peasants and other people working in rural areas was highlighted by the HRC Advisory Committee on the advancement of the rights of peasants and other people working in rural areas (HRC(b), 2012). These issues are being addressed in the newly adopted United Nations declaration on the rights of peasants and other people working in rural areas.

The VGGT emphasize that people: 'can be condemned to a life of hunger and poverty if they lose their tenure rights to their homes, land, fisheries and forests and their livelihoods because of corrupt tenure practices or if implementing agencies fail to protect their tenure rights' (Preface). UNGP 24 requires business enterprises to prioritize the prevention and mitigation of those adverse human rights impacts that are 'most severe or where delayed response would make them irremediable'.

---

[13] Adopted 14 November 2017, part of the campaign is to ensure women have access to 30 per cent of documented land rights compared to the current 4 per cent, https://au.int/ar/newsevents/20171113/african-union-set-launch-gender-and-development-initiative-africa.

A guide on the dual responsibilities of private sector lawyers in advising on the acquisition of land and natural resources

---

Box 1.1 Factors indicating the particular need for careful scrutiny of investments

Investments involving access to rights over, or the acquisition of, large areas of land warrant a high degree of scrutiny in order to ensure that rights, including tenure rights and associated human rights, are respected, as indicated in technical guidance on the VGGT and CFS-RAI:

Some forms of investment, particularly those that involve access to large areas of land, require careful scrutiny as they may result in people being dispossessed of their land…

…Proposals for agricultural investments that require the expropriation of land should be viewed with caution (FAO, 2015).

Legal advice relating to agribusiness investments should reflect the need for careful scrutiny and caution highlighted in the VGGT. Particular caution and scrutiny should be exercised in the context of the allocation of public land and investment proposals which affect land which is used by those with customary tenure rights or those from vulnerable communities such as those with limited access to legal redress (FAO, 2015). Similar issues have been raised by the Special Rapporteur on the Right to Food in relation to the fisheries sector (2012).

The UN Office of the High Commissioner for Human Rights (OHCHR) has also flagged up the risks posed by agribusiness investment in new (greenfield) land for agricultural activities:

…This land may be inhabited or used by communities for their livelihoods, whether or not they are recognized as having legal title. This creates a particular risk for the right of the individuals concerned to an adequate standard of living. (OHCHR, 2012).

In line with that approach, the prevention and mitigation of the impacts of large-scale land acquisitions which are likely to result in adverse impacts on the food security and livelihoods of vulnerable communities should be a priority. Such impacts can have potentially irreversible effects, including the permanent loss of access to natural resources such as grazing, water and forage, as well as land. The possibility of forced evictions and disproportionate action in the context of removals would also make this a priority area for prevention and mitigation, as discussed further below.

Lawyers advising on such proposed investments or transactions are therefore engaging in an area where careful scrutiny and caution, with a view to the protection of rights, is called for. This should be applied from the earliest stages in such transactions, including in initial engagement with the client as discussed in Section 2.

The adverse impacts on human rights of expropriation of community lands for commercial investment have been highlighted by FAO and others (HRC, 2012(a)).[14] As indicated in technical guidance:

Evidence indicates that it is very difficult to expropriate land without having negative impacts on tenure rights and human rights, and expropriation has caused a significant number of land-related disputes (FAO, 2015).

For that reason, the technical guidance recommends avoiding expropriation, where this cannot be avoided, separate guidance on compulsory acquisition has been published.[15]

---

[14] See also Oxfam, 2011.

[15] Guidance on how governments can equitably acquire land for development can be found in FAO's guide on *Compulsory acquisition of land and compensation* (FAO, 2008).

In the light of these current trends and concerns, it is clear that a high degree of scrutiny and caution is advisable, and this should be reflected in the advice and support provided to businesses engaged in the agribusiness sector by their legal advisors, whether in-house or external. Human rights due diligence is of central importance in this regard, as recognized by the IBA:

> Human rights due diligence means that a business should map its human rights risks by severity and likelihood. Through its own activities and its business relationships, a business can impact the rights of various different stakeholders, such as …local communities around its operations. Some of those stakeholders may belong to potentially marginalised or vulnerable groups, who may sometimes be the least visible or vocal in a society, and as a result, could experience more severe negative impacts… (IBA, 2016(a), section 2.3.2.4 citing UNGP 18).

Due diligence is addressed in more detail in Section 3 of this guide.

1.3   LEGAL STATUS AND KEY PRINCIPLES OF THE VGGT AND CFS-RAI

1.3.1   Legal status of the VGGT and CFS-RAI

The VGGT state that they are voluntary (para. 2.1) and, as is also clear from the language used ('should' rather than 'shall'), the VGGT is not a binding treaty. They are however related to binding norms of international law, in particular human rights law. Paragraph 2.2 of the VGGT provides:

> These Guidelines should be *interpreted and applied consistent with existing obligations under national and international law*, and with due regard to voluntary commitments under applicable regional and international instruments. They are *complementary to, and support, national, regional and international initiatives that address human rights and provide secure tenure rights* to land, fisheries and forests, and also initiatives to improve governance. *Nothing in these Guidelines should be read as limiting or undermining any legal obligations to which a State may be subject under international law.*

This means that the VGGT should be interpreted and applied consistently with human rights associated with tenure rights, including the human right to life, to food and to health and the principle of non-discrimination. A breach of the standards laid down in the VGGT is not *per se* a breach of human rights law, but it may indicate that a breach of human rights law is occurring or is likely because the impacts of the breach (such as a failure to recognize customary rights of tenure) leads, or is likely to lead, to a breach of human rights (for example by reason of forced evictions or loss of livelihood). As indicated in FAO technical guidance, the VGGT are:

> …strongly rooted in existing international human rights law, laying out the obligations and responsibilities of state and non-state actors to govern tenure of land, fisheries and forests responsibly, including commons. They provide internationally agreed guidance on how to recognize, protect and support legitimate tenure rights, including individual and collective tenure rights, and those employed under customary systems (FAO, 2016(a)).

Those providing legal advice in the context of transactions relating to the acquisition of land and rights over land will need to consider the potential legal risks arising out of a breach of tenure rights in the light of the VGGT, taking into account the risk of human rights violations. For that reason, this guide refers to a breach of tenure rights 'and associated human rights' to reflect the close relationship between dispossession of tenure rights over land and the risk of, and occurrence of, human rights violations.

DUE DILIGENCE, TENURE AND AGRICULTURAL INVESTMENT

A guide on the dual responsibilities of private sector lawyers in advising on the acquisition of land and natural resources

The CFS-RAI are also voluntary and non-binding, but, as with the VGGT, they are to be interpreted and applied consistently with existing obligations under national and international law, with due regard to voluntary commitments under applicable regional and international instruments. Nothing in the CFS-RAI should be read as limiting or undermining any legal obligations to which a State may be subject under international law (p.6). Each of the principles set out in the CFS-RAI contributes to food security and nutrition, though not every principle may be relevant to every investment.

A range of human rights are highlighted in the CFS-RAI. The CFS-RAI refer extensively to the human right to adequate food in the context of national food security (see, for example, p.11 and p.20) as laid down, in particular, in Article 26 of the International Covenant of Economic, Social and Cultural Rights (ICESCR, 1966), as well as to the Voluntary Guidelines to support the Progressive Realization of the Right to Adequate Food in the context of national Food Security adopted by FAO in 2004. Principle 2 of the CFS-RAI addresses labour rights and rights at work as protected under the conventions of the International Labour Organisation (ILO). Gender equality and non-discrimination are addressed in Principle 3 and respect for legitimate tenure rights to land, fisheries, and forests, as well as existing and potential water uses is addressed in Principle 5, which refers directly to the VGGT and to the Voluntary Guidelines for Securing Sustainable Small-Scale Fisheries in the Context of Food Security and Poverty Eradication (SSF Guidelines). Both instruments lay emphasis on these human rights, among others.[16]

As already indicated, some states have adopted laws which strengthen the legal recognition of customary rights but others have not (Cotula, 2016). The extent to which international human rights laws and standards are directly applicable in the host State, or in the State of establishment of the law firm or client concerned, will depend on relevant national law. However, as indicated in technical guidance for investors, while investors must always comply with national and international law, there will be circumstances where it will be necessary and prudent to go beyond the minimum required by law, as set forth in the VGGT (FAO, 2016). The VGGT, which were adopted unanimously by the CFS, can be regarded as expressing the international consensus on best practice in relation to the governance of tenure (Cotula, 2017(a)).The VGGT should be considered alongside the UNGP, which set a minimum standard for business legitimacy in the context of respect for human rights (OHCHR, 2012) and which indicate that businesses should seek ways to honour the principles of internationally recognized human rights, even when faced with conflicting requirements (UNGP 23(b)). This is further reinforced by OHCHR guidance on the UNGP: 'The responsibility to respect human rights is not, however, limited to compliance with such domestic law provisions. It exists over and above legal compliance'. (OHCHR, 2012).

Those advising businesses are also advised to adopt this approach in technical guidance issued by FAO:

> Business lawyers may be advised to counsel their clients that it is both prudent and ethical to undertake actions that exceed their minimum legal obligations (FAO, 2016(b)).

The extent to which a violation of tenure rights also constitutes a breach of international human rights law will depend on a range of factors including the facts of the case, the human rights instruments to which the host State is party and potentially those to which the investor's State of origin is party. Examples of possible breaches are set out in Section 3, but where the impacts on food security, livelihood and standard of living are significant, where there is discrimination, where forced evictions are threatened or have occurred, or where there is harassment against existing land users or those seeking to protect their rights, these are all are strong indications that human rights violations may be occurring or may be a significant risk.

---

[16] See also OECD/FAO, 2016, p.26 and p.54-55

Box 1.2 Relevant human rights standards

Sources for international human rights standards relevant to the implementation of the VGGT and CFS-RAI include:

- The United Nations Charter (UNC)
- The Universal Declaration on Human Rights (UDHR)
- The International Covenant on Civil and Political Rights (ICCPR)
- The International Covenant on Economic, Social and Cultural Rights (ICESCR)
- The International Convention on the Elimination of All Forms of Racial Discrimination(CERD)
- The Convention on the Elimination of Discrimination against Women (CEDAW)
- The Convention on the Rights of the Child (CRC)
- The Convention on the Rights of Persons with Disabilities (CRPD)
- International Labour Organization Convention (No. 169) concerning Indigenous and Tribal Peoples in Independent Countries
- The UN Declaration on the Rights of Indigenous Peoples (UNDRIP)
- The International Labour Organization Declaration on the Fundamental Principles and Rights at Work

The VGGT refer explicitly to the UDHR, ILO Convention No. 169 and UNDRIP and to 'other international human rights instruments'. The CFS-RAI refer to the UDHR and 'other relevant international human rights instruments'. The OECD/FAO Guidance refers to a range of international human rights instruments, including those listed above. The SSF Guidelines refer to the ICESCR, CEDAW and the relevant conventions of the ILO.

International human rights reflected in the VGGT and CFS-RAI include the right to food, the right to life and to health, labour rights, the principles of equality and non-discrimination, the rights of indigenous and tribal peoples to their ancestral land, including the right of FPIC, and general rights of participation and consultation. The VGGT state that the governance of tenure of land, fisheries and forests should not only take into account rights that are directly linked to access and use of land, fisheries and forests, but also all civil, political, economic, social and cultural rights.

It is therefore clear from the terms of the VGGT, CFS-RAI and the OECD/FAO Guidance that, in the context of agribusiness investment and its potential impacts, the protection of, and respect for, these internationally recognized human rights is closely tied to the protection of the tenure rights referred to in the VGGT.

1.3.2 Legitimate tenure rights

The VGGT are intended to 'contribute to the global and national efforts towards the eradication of hunger and poverty...with the recognition of the centrality of land to development by promoting secure tenure rights and equitable access to land, fisheries and forests'. The importance of small holders in contributing to food security is emphasized in the VGGT and in the CFS-RAI. The primary objective of the VGGT is to improve the governance of tenure of land, fisheries and forests for the benefit of all with an emphasis on vulnerable and marginalised people (VGGT).

A guide on the dual responsibilities of private sector lawyers in advising on the acquisition of land and natural resources

---

Box 1.3 Defining tenure

Tenure is the way that land, fisheries and forests are held or owned by individuals, families, companies or groups. Tenure can encompass diverse "bundles of rights"; for example, the rights to occupy, use, develop, enjoy and withdraw benefits from the natural resources in question; the right to restrict others' access to these resources; and/or the right to manage, sell or bequeath the resources (FAO, 2016(b)).

Customary tenure may be defined as the local rules, institutions and practices governing land, fisheries and forests that have, over time and use, gained social legitimacy and become embedded in the fabric of a society. Although customary rules are not often written down, they may enjoy widespread social sanction and may be generally adhered to by members of a local population (FAO, 2016(b)).

Customary systems may be traditional or indigenous, they may be democratic or hierarchical, they may be transboundary and cross international borders and there may be different systems even within one country. Customary governance systems are not always inclusive and accountable, but are sometimes highly unequal with regard to gender and corrupted by local elites (FAO, 2016(a)).

The VGGT call on States to define the categories of rights that are considered legitimate.

Based on an examination of tenure rights in line with national law, States should provide legal recognition for legitimate tenure rights not currently protected by law. Policies and laws that ensure tenure rights should be non-discriminatory and gender sensitive. Consistent with the principles of consultation and participation of the Guidelines, states should define 'through widely publicized rules' the categories of rights that are considered legitimate.

Accordingly, the VGGT call both on states and on non-State actors, including business enterprises, to respect legitimate tenure rights. States should safeguard legitimate tenure rights 'against all threats and infringements and they should take reasonable measures to identify, record and respect legitimate tenure right holders' (VGGT General Principle (GP) 3A.3.1.1 and 3.1.2, FAO, 2012). None-State actors, including business enterprises:

> …have a responsibility to respect human rights and legitimate tenure rights. Business enterprises should act with due diligence to avoid infringing on the human rights and legitimate tenure rights of others (FAO, 2012).

CFS-RAI Principle 5 defines responsible investment in agriculture as that which respects legitimate tenure rights, in line with the VGGT and the SSF Guidelines.

As indicated in the VGGT, many tenure problems arise because of weak governance. The UN Sustainable Development Goals (SDGs) Agenda 2030 address this issue in the context of eliminating poverty. SDG 1 Target 1.4 sets the following goal:

> By 2030, ensure that all men and women, in particular the poor and vulnerable, have equal rights to economic resources, as well as access to basic services, ownership and control over land and other forms of property, inheritance, natural resources, appropriate new technology and financial services, including microfinance (UN, 2015).

SDG Indicator 1.4.2 has been set to measure the proportion of the total adult population with secure tenure rights to land. SDG 5 addresses gender equality and includes target 5.a addressing reforms to give women access to ownership and control over land and natural resources. Indicators are set for this target (Indicator 5.a.1 and Indicator 5.a.2).[17] These SDG indicators facilitate the tracking of land governance globally and reflect the ongoing international scrutiny to which the protection of tenure is subject within the context of eliminating poverty and addressing gender inequality. This data, which will be publically available, can inform legal risk assessment. Lawyers should make this context clear in advising investor clients on the implications of the impact of investments on tenure. This is addressed further in Section 2.

As explained in technical guidance issued by FAO, the most challenging scenarios are those where there are overlapping tenure rights to the same land (FAO, 2016). This can arise where the State is the legal owner of land over which communities may have longstanding customary rights of use and both the State and the customary users have tenure rights that may be considered to be legitimate. This raises the question of which land tenure rights are 'legitimate' for the purposes of the VGGT. The VGGT do not provide a definitive answer, but they do define the process for determining which tenure rights are legitimate. This should include 'legal protection against forced evictions that are inconsistent with States' existing obligations under national and international law, and against harassment and other threats' (VGGT). FAO technical guidance indicates that all tenure rights formally recognized in law, as well as customary or informal rights not formally recognized but seen as legitimate and practised by communities for a significant period of time, 'should be accepted as legitimate by investors as they carry out their due diligence and project development' (FAO, 2016 and 2016(b)).

Even where statutory systems recognize customary rights, these systems are often inaccessible to local communities due to high access costs and inadequate government capacities to implement and enforce legislation, among other factors (FAO, 2016(a)). Commentators have highlighted that the difficulty in protecting customary rights at the national level needs to be taken into account by those advising on transactions:

> Lawyers need to bear in mind the risk that customary rights will not be protected under national law as the extent to which customary rights are recognised under national law varies considerably depending on the context and jurisdiction, with a tendency for such rights to be categorised as use rights rather than property rights (Cotula, 2016).

It has further been pointed out in technical guidance that:

> In many settings, the interaction of formal and customary systems causes confusion, tension and disputes with regard to rights and access to land. An investor ignores them at his or her peril (FAO, 2016).

1.3.3 Promotion of responsible investment

The concept of responsible investment builds on and expands beyond the concept of legitimate tenure rights. Paragraph 12.4 of the VGGT sets out the criteria for responsible investment:

> Responsible investments should do no harm, safeguard against dispossession of legitimate tenure right holders and environmental damage, and should respect human rights. Such investments should be made working in partnership with relevant levels of government and local holders of tenure rights to land, fisheries and forests, respecting their legitimate tenure rights.

---

[17] Work on developing and operating the indicator is ongoing, see http://www.fao.org/3/a-i6919e.pdf.

DUE DILIGENCE, TENURE AND AGRICULTURAL INVESTMENT

A guide on the dual responsibilities of private sector lawyers in advising on the acquisition of land and natural resources

The VGGT go on to address what responsible investment in agriculture and food systems should strive to do in terms of supporting national and international policy objectives, including the eradication of poverty, the realisation of food security, nutrition and sustainable development (section 12).

The objective of the CFS-RAI is to promote responsible investment in agriculture and food systems that contribute to food security and nutrition, thus supporting the progressive realization of the right to adequate food in the context of national food security.[18] The CFS-RAI build on the VGGT and address areas that are relevant to investment throughout the food system, including labour rights and food loss and waste. The CFS-RAI Principles refer to the VGGT on all areas related to land tenure. In particular, Principle 5 of the CFS-RAI provides that responsible investment in agriculture and food systems respects legitimate tenure rights to land, fisheries, and forests, as well as existing and potential water uses, in line with the VGGT and the SSF Guidelines (FAO, 2014).

The CFS-RAI are addressed, inter alia, to businesses involved in agriculture and food systems which should apply the Principles with a focus on mitigating and managing risks to maximize positive, and avoiding negative, impacts on food security and nutrition, relevant to their context and circumstances. They state that businesses should respect legitimate tenure rights in line with the VGGT and have a responsibility to comply with national laws and regulations and any applicable international law, and to act with due diligence to avoid infringing on human rights.

As indicated in technical guidance on the VGGT, investing responsibly goes far beyond traditional CSR practices seeking: 'not only to avoid negative social and environmental impacts, but also to create mutually beneficial economic relationships with the affected communities' (FAO, 2016).

---

[18] The CFS-RAI Principles and the VGGT are therefore complementary tools for addressing responsible investment in agriculture and food systems, (FAO, 2015, p. 7).

DUAL ROLE AND RESPONSIBILITIES OF PRIVATE SECTOR LAWYERS

2. DUAL ROLE AND RESPONSIBILITIES OF PRIVATE SECTOR LAWYERS

2.1 RESPECTING HUMAN RIGHTS IS A CORPORATE RESPONSIBILITY FOR LAW FIRMS AND THEIR CLIENTS

UNGP 11 states that:

> Business enterprises should respect human rights. This means that they should avoid infringing on the human rights of others and should address adverse human rights impacts with which they are involved.

This responsibility[19] applies to all types of business enterprises, wherever they operate. Accordingly, the UNGP apply directly to law firms, as well as to their business clients. As one commentator on the UNGP has pointed out, in the context of their implications for corporate lawyers: managing a company's risk of adverse human rights impacts is required for prudent corporate governance and risk management (Sherman, 2013).

Law firms increasingly recognise the importance of their own responsibilities under the UNGP, in particular by referring to them in high level policy statements. The operational integration of UNGP standards into all aspect of the work of the firm may be less easy to determine however.[20] This contrasts with areas where domestic legislation explicitly requires steps to be taken by businesses, including certain law firms, such as the United Kingdom's Modern Slavery Act 2015.[21] An increasing number of States and sub-state legislatures, including those of France and California have adopted domestic legislation requiring businesses to undertake due diligence and ensure transparency in their supply chains, including in the context of modern slavery, so this can be seen as a growing trend towards national legislation requiring adherence to UNGP and thus making aspects of the UNGP legally binding at the national level. Private sector lawyers should alert clients to the increasing likelihood that national laws will reflect these international standards and that non-compliance with the UNGP standards will be seen as illegitimate even where not directly required under national law.

Anecdotal evidence suggests that responsibility for UNGP implementation tends to fall within the CSR responsibilities assigned to particular partners of law firms rather than necessarily (also) being the explicit responsibility of each department. To the extent that this is the case, this approach may not be enough to ensure that issues related to the protection of legitimate tenure rights and related human rights are addressed effectively in all relevant departments in the context of large scale land transactions. Whilst litigation departments in law firms will generally have to address the dispute resolution and dispute settlement implications of the UNGP (this is explored further in Section 3), other departments engaged in the transactional

---

[19] As John Ruggie has stated: 'In human rights discourse, respecting rights means to not infringe on the rights of others. We know that the corporate responsibility to respect human rights is a transnational social norm because the relevant actors acknowledge it as such, including businesses themselves in their corporate responsibility commitments' (Ruggie, 2017, p.14).

[20] As noted by John Ruggie in 2017, implementation of the UNGP generally is partial but not yet deep enough, (Ruggie, 2017, p.19), referring to the analysis set out in Shift, 'Human Rights Reporting: Are Companies Telling Investors What They Need To Know? (2017), available at https://www.shiftproject.org/resources/publications/corporate-human-rights-reporting-maturity/, accessed 8 June 2017.

[21] Section 54 of the Act requires any commercial organisation which supplies goods or services, carries on a business or part of a business in the UK, and whose annual turnover is £36m or above, to produce a statement for each financial year describing the steps the commercial organisation has taken during the financial year to ensure that slavery and human trafficking is not taking place in any of its supply chains, and in any part of its own business. Alternatively, a statement can simply state that the organisation has taken no such steps, see Law Society of England and Wales Practice Note dated 6 December 2016 https://www.lawsociety.org.uk/support-services/advice/practice-notes/modern-slavery-act-and-section-54/.

DUE DILIGENCE, TENURE AND AGRICULTURAL INVESTMENT

A guide on the dual responsibilities of private sector lawyers in advising on the acquisition of land and natural resources

side of large-scale land acquisition may not be as focussed on these standards, for example in the drafting of contracts, or in supporting impact assessment and consultation processes and negotiating with stakeholders.

A broader and deeper engagement with the UNGP and specifically with tenure and associated human rights is required to ensure that issues arising from these standards are addressed at an operational level. This might be facilitated by partners heading a broader range of departments taking joint responsibility for UNGP implementation where this is not already the case. The breadth of engagement is also likely to require comprehensive internal training across all departments of law firms.

Assessment of legal risk is an area where engagement with the UNGP generally, and with the protection of tenure rights and associated human rights in particular, can be addressed effectively. This is an area where the concepts of the role of the 'wise counsellor' and leverage, as highlighted recently by the IBA, are particularly relevant, as discussed below.

As recognised by the IBA, there are numerous legal practice areas in which legal advice and services 'can shape a business client's ability to respect human rights'(IBA, 2016) The Reference Annex to the IBA Guide notes that the UNGPs:

> …now provide, for the first time, an authoritative global framework and methodology for advising business clients on how to mitigate or avoid involvement in adverse human rights impacts (IBA, 2016(a)).

The Law Society of England and Wales has noted that human rights are relevant to solicitors and law firms as legal service providers and as businesses in their own right (Law Society, 2016). The Law Society has recommended that firms may wish to do the following:

> Conduct a human rights due diligence on their clients in addition to complying with applicable regulatory requirements concerning, for example, conflicts of interest and anti-money laundering;
>
> Identify potential human rights related risks associated with the client and its instructions and discuss these with colleagues and the client, as required;
>
> Raise and explore with the client human rights issues that may be relevant to the legal advice required; and
>
> Integrate any potential outcomes of the human rights due diligence into retention letters, legal advice and case management (Law Society of England and Wales, 2016).

The Law Society of England and Wales also notes that, in relation to advising clients on the human rights impacts of their activities:

> It is possible that, unless specifically instructed as part of their retainer, solicitors would not consider themselves instructed, empowered or competent in the context of the particular client relationship to advise on non-legal risks. It is, however, well established that where in the course of taking instructions a solicitor learns of facts which reveal the existence of obvious risks, the solicitor is required to do more than merely advise within the strict limits of the retainer (Law Society of England and Wales, 2016).

The focus of this guide is on the UNGP, together with the VGGT, CFS-RAI and OECD/FAO Guidance, but similar considerations apply in relation to other international frameworks for corporate responsibility, including the UN Global Compact,[22] the 2011 OECD Guidelines

---

[22] The Global Compact adopted in 2000 lays down 10 principles which companies are asked to embrace and support including Principle 1 calling on businesses to support and respect the protection of internationally proclaimed human rights and Principle 2 which calls on businesses to make sure they are not complicit in human rights abuses, see https://www.unglobalcompact.org/what-is-gc/mission/principles.

for Multinational Enterprises (the OECD Guidelines) and the ISO 26-000 Guidance on Social Responsibility. Regional and national frameworks and professional standards support the UNGP and are also relevant, as discussed below.

2.1.1 Dual responsibilities

The IBA has confirmed that neither the UNGPs nor the IBA Practical Guide (IBA, 2016) are intended to override the professional standards of any jurisdiction or to prescribe any of the factors that lawyers may or may not consider as independent professionals (IBA Resolution 2016). However, the IBA has affirmed that the UNGPs may nevertheless be 'highly relevant' to the advice or services to be rendered the client:

> …where they are within the agreed scope of services (or mandate) to be provided (which may include a range of services, from very specific to highly general); where they are reflected or incorporated in relevant laws, or where they are permitted or encouraged to be considered by lawyers in their independent judgement under applicable professional standards of conduct (IBA, 2016).

The specific duties of law firms under the UNGP arise in the wider context of ongoing debate as to the ethical obligations of lawyers (see Luban and Wendel, 2017).[23] The IBA has advised that Bar Associations may wish to consider drawing to their members' attention the ethical considerations which a lawyer should take into account in the field of business and human rights when advising clients (IBA, 2015).

Advocates for International Development (A41D), a pro bono organisation in the United Kingdom, has undertaken an analysis of the relationship between the UNGP and codes of professional conduct for the legal profession in a range of national jurisdictions (A4ID, 2013). A4ID found areas where such codes support the UNGP and areas where there is tension between the UNGP and some professional codes. Only one code (South Africa) was found to specifically mention human rights. As noted in the A41D report, the commentary to the 2006 Charter of Core Principles of the European Legal Profession acknowledged that those principles take into account international human rights instruments (A4ID, 2013).[24] The report also notes that the American Bar Association (ABA) adopted a resolution in 2012 endorsing the UNGP and urging the legal community to integrate the UNGP into their operations and practices.

For the purposes of this guide, the guidance issued by the IBA, the commentaries on the UNGP and the technical guidance issued by the FAO on the implementation of the VGGT, in particular, are all considered helpful in clarifying the duties of law firms in this area.

UNGP 13 sets out the types of requirements placed on businesses by virtue of their responsibility to respect human rights. Businesses must:

(a) avoid causing or contributing to adverse human rights impacts through their own activities, and addressing such impacts when they occur;

(b) seek to prevent or mitigate adverse human rights impacts that are directly linked to their operations, products or services by their business relationships, even if they have not contributed to those impacts.

---

[23] Luban and Wendel discuss the critique of the standard neutral partisanship conception and the emergence of arguments in favour of a more public spirited role requiring fidelity to the law as an operating principle (Luban and Wendel, 2017).

[24] Charter of Core Principles of the European Legal Profession (2006) http://www.ccbe.eu/fileadmin/user_upload/NTCdocument/EN_Code_of_conductp1_1306748215.pdf

DUE DILIGENCE, TENURE AND AGRICULTURAL INVESTMENT

A guide on the dual responsibilities of private sector lawyers in advising on the acquisition of land and natural resources

The commentary to UNGP 13 indicates that business enterprises may be involved with adverse human rights impacts, either through their own activities or as a result of their business relationships with other parties (OHCHR, 2012).

If at risk of causing or contributing to adverse impacts, a business should cease or change its conduct and remediate any adverse impact. If linked to an adverse impact on human rights, it has a responsibility to use its leverage to encourage the entity that caused or contributed to the impact to prevent or mitigate its recurrence. The concept of leverage is discussed further below.

> If a law firm does not conduct human rights diligence in respect of the way in which it provides legal services to clients, it would seem highly likely that there is a real risk that it will have contributed to the impacts caused by the client.

In the context of UNGP 13, it may be thought that a law firm is more likely to contribute or to be 'directly linked' to impacts rather than causing them, on the basis that the client is directing the transaction and providing instructions on what is to be addressed by the law firm. However, if a law firm deliberately omits consideration of, or agrees not to address, tenure rights and associated human rights in the context of advising on a large-scale land acquisition, either at all or in part (for example by not addressing the impacts on local indigenous peoples or on food security), the question arises as to whether the firm is thereby causing or 'contributing' to impacts, rather than being directly linked to them. It is relevant in this context that law firms, as well as their business clients, are directly bound by the human rights due diligence obligation set out in UNGP 17. Due diligence is examined in Section 3. If a law firm does not conduct human rights diligence in respect of the way in which it provides legal services to clients, it would seem highly likely that there is a real risk that it will have contributed to the impacts caused by the client. If a firm knowingly supports or facilitates action to avoid the application of national safeguards protecting tenure rights, that would also appear likely to constitute a contribution to any impact. This could arise in the context of advising on the parcelling of land into separate smaller acquisitions so as to fall below a protected threshold for land purchase aimed at protecting tenure rights. The risk of causing or contributing to adverse human rights impacts in such a case would appear to be extremely high.

The implications of 'contributing to' an impact, rather than being directly linked to it within the terms of the UNGP, are that the firm should then take steps to 'cease and prevent' the impact, in addition to using leverage to mitigate it. These steps could include proactively raising the issue with the client and considering whether the firm can continue to act if directed not to address the issues of the protection of tenure rights and associated human rights in advising on or supporting the transaction (for example in the way that contracts are drafted). Firms will need to act in conformity with professional rules and take account of engagement letters with the particular client in this regard.

There is therefore a dual, but closely connected, responsibility for private sector lawyers engaged in work that relates to investments and land transactions which may impact on tenure rights. In their work with clients, private sector lawyers need to: (1) consider how their professional obligations are affected by the standards laid down in the VGGT and CFS-RAI, and (2) consider how these standards are relevant to their firm's CSR commitments, as well as to their clients' compliance with the UNGP. There is a close relationship between these two roles and sets of responsibilities. The Reference Annex to the IBA Guide states that:

> For a law firm, the primary focus of the [due diligence] assessment would be on future potential risks, since — as noted above — the UNGPs do not restrict the right of businesses to robustly defend legal claims that they violated human rights...(IBA, 2016(a)).

However, law firms will need to be both proactive and reactive in addressing risks and should continuously monitor their own systems for ensuring compliance with the UNGP in this context, particularly given the specific risks posed by weak governance of tenure rights, the vulnerability of those who may be affected, and the severity of the adverse impacts on human rights which may result from their breach, as highlighted in the VGGT and CFS-RAI.

It will be helpful for law firms to identify risks at the outset of the client relationship (IBA, 2016(a)) so as to ensure that the relationship with the client is based on a full understanding of the potential issues and the way these may impact on the type and scope of advice that may be required in this area. This is also important for the law firm as it may be difficult to withdraw from the relationship at a later stage, as discussed in the IBA Practical Guide (see below).

Neither the VGGT, the CFS-RAI nor the OECD/FAO Guidance specifically address the role or responsibilities of law firms in this area. However, all three instruments emphasise: (1) the importance of the rule of law for all actors, including non-State actors, involved in agricultural investment and transactions impacting on tenure rights; and (2) the specific duties of business enterprises to support the standards set out in those instruments. The first of these is discussed below and the second in Section 3.

2.1.2 Upholding the rule of law

In relation to the rule of law, all three instruments are explicit. CFS-RAI Principle 9 addresses respect for the rule and application of the law. The CFS-RAI also state that business enterprises 'have a responsibility to comply with national laws and regulations and any applicable international law, and act with due diligence to avoid infringing on human rights'.

The VGGT explicitly affirm the rule of law as a 'principle of implementation'; that is, an essential principle to be followed in implementing the Guidelines (para. 3B.7). The VGGT also refer to compliance with national law in the context of responsible investment (para. 12.1). The OECD/ FAO Guidance emphasises compliance by businesses with national and international law in respect of human rights, tenure rights and governance in its model enterprise policy for responsible agricultural supply chains.[25]

A number of codes of professional conduct refer to the role or obligation of lawyers to uphold the rule of law. However, in recent analysis conducted by A4ID, only a few codes addressed the conflicting duties of lawyers in the context of considering the duties to clients and the responsibility to respect human rights (2013). In the context of advising on the impacts of large scale land acquisitions, these issues may arise and will need to be addressed having regard to international guidance on tenure rights and associated human rights, as well as relevant professional codes. Law firms may wish to clarify which international and national laws and standards are likely to be relevant in this area when they agree the scope of their services with clients, including by reference to letters of engagement, this is discussed further below.

---

[25] Defined in the OECD/FAO Guidance as the system encompassing all the activities, organisations, actors, technology, information, resources and services involved in producing agri-food products for consumer markets including upstream and downstream sectors from the supply of agricultural inputs to production, post-harvest handling, processing, transportation, marketing, distribution, and retailing as well as support services, OECD/FAO, 2016 at page 19 and Fig.1.1.

DUE DILIGENCE, TENURE AND AGRICULTURAL INVESTMENT

A guide on the dual responsibilities of private sector lawyers in advising on the acquisition of land and natural resources

Adherence to upholding the rule of law does not mean adopting a narrow approach to the scope of advice however. As one leading commentator has suggested:

> UN Guiding Principle 19 and ABA Model Rule 2.1 should be read in harmony. Both require lawyers to offer advice beyond determining the letter of the law; the advice should encompass potential human rights infringements and the full range of other legal and business consequences that may likely result, and it should suggest how to achieve a client's goals in a way that respects human rights (Sherman, 2013).

UNGP 23(a) emphasises the importance of legal compliance. It states that business enterprises should 'comply with all applicable laws and respect internationally recognised human rights, wherever they operate'. However, where national law is in tension with internationally recognised human rights, the UNGPs state that a business should strive to honour the principles of internationally recognised human rights 'to the greatest extent possible' without violating applicable laws (cited in IBA, 2016). Guidance issued by the OHCHR states:

> If there is a direct conflict of requirements, the challenge is to find ways of honouring the principles of internationally recognized rights (OHCHR, 2012).

In order to meet these requirements to provide relevant context for advice by reference to the principle of the rule of law, and to honour the principles of international human rights law so far as possible, it is clearly necessary to advise on the application and scope of international human rights law, as it relates to the client's business and specific investment in this area.

Businesses should not attempt to take advantage of weak legal frameworks in countries that insufficiently protect human rights in order to lower their own standards. This is relevant to law firms as well as their clients. The Reference Annex to the IBA Guidance states that:

> ....the absence of national laws on human rights or a failure in their enforcement does not limit the businesses' responsibility to respect human rights (IBA, 2016(a)).

> ...where laws do not adequately protect human rights, where they are ambiguous or where the future evolution of the law or its enforcement is uncertain, clients may wish for guidance from their lawyers on how to conduct business in order to mitigate or avoid involvement in such harm. The business case for providing such guidance is particularly strong where the risks of human rights impacts are severe (IBA, 2016).

The risk of severe impacts in the context of large-scale acquisition of land or long-term rights to land is well documented, as set out in Section 1.

2.1.3   Technical expert or wise counsellor?

The wider debate as to the ethical obligations of lawyers, particularly those advising corporations, has led to calls for lawyers to take on a more proactive role in addressing the potential impacts of actions proposed by the client, including by engaging in dialogue with the client: 'on those occasions when lawful (or arguably lawful) corporate conduct appears to involve moral wrongdoing (or arguable wrongdoing) in relation to third parties or aggregate social concerns (Pepper, 2015). This approach is informed by relative power of the corporation, particularly large multinational corporations, as compared with the vulnerability of those who may be impacted by the corporation's actions. Such an approach is clearly relevant in the context of commercial investment in agriculture in States where tenure protection is weak and those reliant on customary tenure rights for their food security and livelihoods are members of marginalised and vulnerable communities. The suggestion that the lawyer should bring such harms and risk to the attention of the corporate decision-makers and discuss them and alternatives in the light of the 'special power, risks and obligations of the corporate entity' (Pepper, 2015) would clearly bring into play obligations under the UNGP and the international standards set out in the VGGT, as well as the risks of breaching international human rights obligations *per se*.

IBA guidance highlights the potential role of lawyers as 'wise counsellors' advising in a proactive and pre-emptive way:

> As technical experts, lawyers advise business clients on legal risks that arise under applicable laws. As wise counsellors or trusted advisors, lawyers identify and advise on potential legal risks that may likely arise in the future...(IBA, 2016(a)).

> As a technical expert, a lawyer may be asked to exercise his or her expertise, skill and judgment in applying the law to the facts. To do so effectively, a lawyer should understand the UNGPs to see how they shape and influence existing law and regulation and emerging forms of governance. As a wise counsellor or trusted advisor, a lawyer may be asked to provide relevant context in order not only to answer the question of what is legal, but also, what is right and fair in the context of the business' medium to long term interests and sustainability, and what should be done (IBA, 2016(a)).

The relevant context in this area is outlined in Sction 1 and is also relevant to the conduct of human rights due diligence as discussed in Section 3, bearing in mind the specific and well documented risks of human rights breaches associated with the dispossession of land and of rights to use land and natural resources, including fisheries and forests, in the context of the failure to protect legitimate tenure rights. These risks are extensively addressed in technical guidance, together with the means of preventing or mitigating them.

2.1.4 The principle of independence

The principle of independence has been reaffirmed by the IBA (IBA, 2011. IBA, 2016) and is addressed in the Reference Annex to the IBA Guide:

> The principle of legal independence does not preclude or discourage lawyers from taking into account the UNGPs in providing advice and services where they are relevant. Given the shifting boundaries between legal standards and global norms, it may be difficult, as a practical matter, for a lawyer to advise on the former and ignore the latter (IBA, 2016(a)).

2.2 RESPONSIBILITIES OF LAW FIRMS AS BUSINESS ENTERPRISES

The VGGT (12.13) provide that:

> Professionals who provide services to States, investors and holders of tenure rights to land, fisheries and forests should undertake due diligence to the best of their ability when providing their services, irrespective of whether it is specifically requested.

This indicates that lawyers, in the context of providing legal services to investors and holders or acquirers of tenure rights, should undertake due diligence when providing their services. As indicated above, this has a dual aspect: (1) to support the requirements placed directly on clients, under international standards, to conduct due diligence, and (2) to take steps to ensure that the law firm itself is acting with due diligence in respect of the provision of legal services to clients, including at the stage of engagement and continuing thereafter.

The OECD/FAO Guidance highlights its applicability in the context of 'business relationships such as investment funds, sovereign wealth funds or banks'. The Guidance notes that, under the OECD Guidelines, enterprises are expected to 'use their leverage' over entities directly linked to their operations, products or services and that accordingly enterprises 'are expected to use their leverage to support the implementation of the Guidance'. In the context of agricultural supply chains, this clearly has a wide scope, as the definition of a supply chain is comprehensive, although the Guidance indicates that the risks for tenure rights occur primarily at the production stage.

DUE DILIGENCE, TENURE AND AGRICULTURAL INVESTMENT

A guide on the dual responsibilities of private sector lawyers in advising on the acquisition of land and natural resources

2.2.1 Leverage

In the context of the UNGP, 'leverage' is considered to exist where the enterprise has the ability to effect change in the wrongful practices of the entity that causes harm' (commentary to UNGP 19).[26] The OHCHR Interpretative Guide defines leverage as 'an advantage that gives power to influence' (OHCHR, 2012).

The Commentary to the 2011 OECD Guidelines notes that:

> ...there are practical limitations on the ability of enterprises to effect change in the behaviour of their suppliers.... Appropriate responses with regard to the business relationship may include continuation of the relationship with a supplier throughout the course of risk mitigation efforts; temporary suspension of the relationship while pursuing ongoing risk mitigation; or, as a last resort, disengagement with the supplier either after failed attempts at mitigation, or where the enterprise deems mitigation not feasible, or because of the severity of the adverse impact...(OECD, 2011).

The CFS-RAI point to the 'unique' leverage that can be exercised by financial institutions:

> The provision of finance allows these institutions a unique leveraging position where they can communicate with a broad range of stakeholders about their roles, responsibilities, and actions to facilitate implementation of the Principles.

The OHCHR notes that leverage is likely to be influenced by a range of factors including: the terms of the contract between the business and entity; the ability of the enterprise to incentivise human rights performance of an entity; the benefits of working together and the harm if services were to be withdrawn (OHCHR, 2012).

This raises the question as to the nature of the distinct leverage that can be exercised by law firms in this context, given the general expectations referred to above as to the leverage that business entities have over each other and given guidance published by the IBA on the responsibilities of law firms under the UNGP and other frameworks. The IBA has addressed the issue of leverage through the concept of the wise counsellor (discussed above), noting that:

> A law firm's main ability to influence a client to avoid or mitigate human rights impacts not explicitly addressed by hard law may depend largely on whether the client sees the lawyer as a wise professional counsellor or trusted advisor, a status which is not automatically granted (IBA, 2016).

The Guidance from the IBA then indicates a number of steps that firms may take to promote this status with clients including developing internal capacity and identifying where problems have arisen for corporations which have ignored human rights issues (IBA, 2016) Some of these issues are also addressed in Guidance issued by the Council of Bars and Law Societies of Europe (CBBE) (CBBE, 2017).[27]

Leverage may vary from client to client, being affected by a range of factors relating to the firm-client relationship (A4ID, 2013). The exercise of leverage is likely to entail proactive engagement by the firm from the outset of the relationship with the client in raising the issue of tenure rights and associated human rights with the client, offering to advise on the legal implications of potential impacts and informing the client that, in the light of the UNGP, the VGGT, CFS-RAI and other relevant international standards, such advice is required in any event, whether or not

---

[26] See also OECD/FAO, 2016, at page 21 and see OECD, 2011, p24 and p33.

[27] The CCBE represents the Bars and Law Societies of 32 countries (including the 28 EU Member States and Norway, Iceland, Liechtenstein and Switzerland) and a further 13 associate and observer countries, and through them more than 1 million European lawyers, (CBBE, 2017, Preamble).

provided directly by the firm. The firm can alert the client to the implications of not seeking and acting upon such advice in terms of reputational risk, financial risk (FAO, 2016), legal risks and involvement in disputes and the need for remediation if the impacts are not prevented or mitigated. Law firms can and should advise on what is in the client's best interests and this would include avoiding and addressing adverse impacts on human rights within the terms of the UNGP, given the risks highlighted above. Under the ABA Model Rules of Professional Conduct, Rule 2.1 provides that in rendering advice: 'a lawyer may refer not only to law but to other considerations such as moral, economic, social, and political factors that may be relevant to the client's situation' (ABA, 2016).

In the event that clients choose not to act upon such advice, firms will need to consider whether to decline or withdraw services (see below), taking into account their professional obligations. This guide does not address potential liabilities of law firms in this context but the IBA Practical Guide concerning liability insurance is of assistance in this area (IBA, 2016).

2.2.2 Withdrawal

In the context of addressing adverse impacts where businesses may be sourcing from, or linked to, any business partner violating legitimate tenure rights, the OECD/FAO Guidance puts the onus on those businesses to work with their business partners on corrective action and 'to the extent possible, terminate the business relationship if no remedial action is taken'.

The commentary to UNGP 19 advises that businesses consider withdrawing from a relationship with a third party in circumstances where a severe negative impact occurs through a business relationship, and continues notwithstanding the business's efforts to influence the third party to cease the conduct. In relation to law firms and independent lawyers, the Reference Annex to the IBA Guide refers to this commentary and states:

> The same applies to law firms and independent lawyers. If, notwithstanding a lawyer's advice, the client continues to engage (or appears likely to continue to engage) in harmful conduct, then the lawyer should consider withdrawal from the relationship, if doing so is legally permissible. Withdrawal is not an automatic conclusion…the decision to terminate a business relationship is a difficult one for any business (IBA, 2016(a)).

The IBA Practical Guide refers to withdrawal as a 'last resort' which, in any event, may not be permitted and states that:

> Staying in the relationship and continuing to try to persuade the client to prevent and mitigate human rights impacts may serve the purposes of the UNGPs better than withdrawal (IBA, 2016).

The recent analysis by A4ID indicates that a number of codes provide for withdrawal for 'good cause' or a compelling reason and the report recommends that that professional bodies consider defining the relevant standard so as to include the client's failure to respect human rights (2013).

2.3 HOW CAN LAWYERS ADDRESS LEGITIMATE HUMAN (TENURE-RELATED) RIGHTS?

2.3.1 High level policy statement

The UNGP provide that businesses should adopt, at a senior level, a human rights policy statement (UNGP 15(a) and 16) which stipulates the enterprise's human rights expectations of personnel, business partners and other parties directly linked to its operations, products or services and

DUE DILIGENCE, TENURE AND AGRICULTURAL INVESTMENT

A guide on the dual responsibilities of private sector lawyers in advising on the acquisition of land and natural resources

is publicly available and is 'communicated internally and externally to all personnel, business partners and other relevant parties'. The statement should also be 'reflected in operational policies and procedures necessary to embed it throughout the business enterprise.'

Many firms have adopted a statement of this kind. A key question will be the extent to which its content is reflected in operational policies and procedures, including those relevant to advising on and assisting with large-scale land acquisitions. In order to ensure that tenure rights and associated human rights are addressed effectively it will be useful to explicitly refer to the VGGT and CFS-RAI in such statements. This does not yet appear to be common practice among law firms however.

The firm may wish to review to what extent it undertakes pro bono work in this area, nevertheless bearing in mind that undertaking pro bono work does not offset a failure to respect human rights elsewhere (UNGP 11 and IBA, 2016(a)).

2.3.2 Engagement letters and contracts with clients

Within the general context of securing consistency between the law firm's own CSR commitment and human rights policy, the specific issue of the VGGT and CFS-RAI standards should be addressed.

Law firms can also signal their knowledge of and commitment to these standards by addressing them in initial discussions as to the potential mandate for legal services and by referring to them in engagement letters. Whilst recognising that these instruments are not per se legally binding (see above), the law firm can signal that they represent an international standard which is related to international human rights laws and which entails a due diligence process which is also mandated by the UNGP. The client's approach to the VGGT and CFS-RAI can also be addressed in the due diligence questionnaire between firm and client. This can inform the initial human rights assessment of a prospective client, perhaps combined with a conflict check (A4ID, 2013).

The business client may ask the law firm to sign their own code of conduct and the approach to tenure rights and associated human rights should also be considered in this context. It has been suggested that in future clients may consider malpractice lawsuits against firms that failed to incorporate business and human rights considerations into specific advice (Law Firm Report, 2016).

Analysis by A4ID indicates that the codes of professional conduct of a number of jurisdictions explicitly provide that lawyers do not have an obligation to accept a client and suggest that, where this is the case, potential human rights impacts could be considered before deciding whether to agree to be retained (2013).

2.3.3 Training

In order to advise on the implications of the VGGT and CFS-RAI standards effectively, lawyers will need to have appropriate expertise on the legal framework for tenure rights and associated human rights and in particular on how these should be integrated into the due diligence process (see Section 3). Law firms may wish to review training provision for tenure rights to see how internal training in these areas compares with other areas such as anti-corruption and modern slavery compliance. Law firms have noted the need for lawyers to be trained to be 'on the look out' for potential human rights risks in the context of client relationships (Law Firm Report, 2016).

In this area, given the extent of technical guidance on tenure and related issues which is available from FAO, the OECD and other bodies, it may be particularly useful for firms to map out the range of guidance, the specific issues addressed and how these relate to each other, and to the key international human rights instruments.

2.4   RELATIONSHIP WITH OTHER AREAS OF REGULATION

In making more explicit reference to the VGGT and CFS-RAI in policy statements and operational guidance to departments, law firms may also wish to review the extent to which other regulatory regimes may be relevant and whether approaches taken in other areas are potentially relevant as indicating good or best practice. Areas of overlap or complementarity include frameworks for transparency and anti-corruption measures. Both these issues are addressed in the VGGT with regard to tenure rights (VGGT).

As underlined in TG No.4, transparency is key to tackling corruption:

> A main reason for promoting transparency in investment promotion, approval and monitoring processes is to address the information asymmetries that may lead to economic inefficiencies and abuses (FAO, 2015).

FAO's technical guidance for investors identifies, as high risk factors for agricultural investment, that the locality where the project may be situated 'has significant corruption, and corrupt activities have been observed in relation to the proposed project', and that joint venture partners or other local partners in the investment have been involved in corrupt activities (FAO, 2016).

The legal regimes addressing corruption which should be adhered to in the context of large-scale land acquisitions include the OECD's 1997 Convention on Combating Bribery of Foreign Public Officials in International Business Transactions, and subsequent Recommendations, and the 2003 UN Convention against Corruption (UNCAC) (see also FAO, 2016). Lawyers should ensure that advice on international anti-corruption regimes, and the national laws which implement them, is incorporated into advising on large-scale land transactions and informs advice on all elements of due diligence, including public participation and consultation.

2.5   LIABILITY OF LAWYERS

The Reference Guide to the IBA Guidance states that the UNGPs:

> ...do not and cannot by themselves impose legal liabilities on any business. This applies to law firms and their lawyers as well as other business enterprises. Nor do they alter professional rules of conduct for lawyers. Significant business risks, legal and otherwise, from involvement in human rights harm *have pre-existed the UNGPs and continue to exist apart from the UNGPs* (IBA, 2016(a)) (emphasis added).

The potential liability for lawyers and law firms who contribute to, or are linked to, human rights breaches goes beyond the scope of this guide. However, the potential for liability has been addressed by commentators and provides a further reason to address international standards relating to respect for tenure rights and associated human rights proactively.

DUE DILIGENCE, TENURE AND AGRICULTURAL INVESTMENT

A guide on the dual responsibilities of private sector lawyers in advising on the acquisition of land and natural resources

The OHCHR has confirmed that enterprises, and this would include law firms, need to 'know and show' the steps they have taken to respect human rights:

> As a legal matter, most national jurisdictions prohibit complicity in the commission of a crime, and a number allow for criminal liability of business enterprises in such cases. Typically, civil actions can also be based on an enterprise's alleged contribution to a harm, although these may not be framed in human rights terms. The weight of international criminal law jurisprudence indicates that the relevant standard for aiding and abetting is knowingly providing practical assistance or encouragement that has a substantial effect on the commission of a crime (OHCHR, 2011).

DUE DILIGENCE AND THE PROTECTION OF LEGITIMATE TENURE RIGHTS AND HUMAN RIGHTS

3. DUE DILIGENCE AND THE PROTECTION OF LEGITIMATE TENURE RIGHTS AND HUMAN RIGHTS

Due diligence should be central to the protection of human rights and associated tenure rights by investors. Lawyers play a key role in advising on and supporting the due diligence process as explained in this Section. Under the dual responsibilities examined in Section 2, lawyers should also conduct internal due diligence of their own operations and it will be important to ensure coherence and consistency between these two aspects of the business and human rights framework.

In order to meet their responsibility to respect human rights, business enterprises should have in place policies and processes 'appropriate to their size and circumstances' which include a human rights due diligence process to identify, prevent, mitigate and account for how they address their impacts on human rights (UNGP 15(b)). The due diligence process should assess actual and potential human rights impacts, integrate and act upon the findings, track responses, and communicate how impacts are addressed (UNGP 17).[28] Human rights due diligence has been described as a dynamic, iterative, and ongoing management process that draws upon established concepts of corporate governance and risk management (Sherman, 2013). A key aspect of human rights due diligence is that it should be ongoing and be applied at every stage of the investment process as well as at every stage of the relationship between lawyer and client.

In the specific context of tenure rights and associated human rights, the VGGT provide that business enterprises should include appropriate risk management systems to prevent and address adverse impacts on human rights and legitimate tenure rights. They should also identify and assess any actual or potential impacts on human rights and legitimate tenure rights in which they may be involved (VGGT).

Box 3.1 VGGT and due diligence

Non-state actors including business enterprises have a responsibility to respect human rights and legitimate tenure rights. Business enterprises should act with due diligence to avoid infringing on the human rights and legitimate tenure rights of others. They should include appropriate risk management systems to prevent and address adverse impacts on human rights and legitimate tenure rights. Business enterprises should provide for and cooperate in non-judicial mechanisms to provide remedy, including effective operational-level grievance mechanisms, where appropriate, where they have caused or contributed to adverse impacts on human rights and legitimate tenure rights. Business enterprises should identify and assess any actual or potential impacts on human rights and legitimate tenure rights in which they may be involved ..." (VGGT).

---

[28] The OECD/FAO Guidance describes due diligence as the process through which enterprises can identify, assess, mitigate, prevent and account for how they address the actual and potential adverse impacts of their activities as an integral part of business decision-making and risk management systems (OECD/FAO, 2016, p.21).

A guide on the dual responsibilities of private sector lawyers in advising on the acquisition of land and natural resources

A combined reading of the UNGP and the VGGT confirms that the human rights impact of agricultural investment should be factored into due diligence processes (FAO, 2016(b)). Law firms will wish to be able to demonstrate that they operate due diligence internally as well as supporting their clients to conduct due diligence. As indicated in the IBA Practical Guide:

> Human rights due diligence is …an ongoing process to enable businesses to 'know and show' that they are addressing their human rights impacts through assessing impacts, taking integrated action in response to identified impacts, and tracking and monitoring, and communicating the company's efforts to address its human rights impacts (IBA, 2016).

As discussed in Section 2, law firms have a dual responsibility under the UNGP. In the context of respecting tenure rights and associated human rights, law firms should: (1) advise and assist their clients in operating a human rights due diligence process in respect of investments in agriculture which may impact on tenure rights, recognising that such impacts may not be easy to determine without thorough investigation; and (2) ensure that they have an internal human rights due diligence process which identifies, mitigates and accounts for their impacts on human rights in this area of work, deploying appropriate resources and relevant expertise and based on a proactive approach (within the constraints of professional rules as discussed in Section 2).

3.1   ASSESSING THE RISK OF ALL POTENTIAL HUMAN RIGHTS VIOLATIONS

Commercial investments which have the effect of depriving or restricting communities' access to land and natural resources pose a significant risk of violations of civil and political as well as economic, social and cultural rights. It will be important that due diligence addresses the full range of relevant human rights. Deprivation of access to land is much more likely where tenure rights, including usage rights, are not securely protected under national law. In order to meet both their own responsibilities under the UNGP, and those of the client, to respect human rights and to avoid and address adverse impacts, lawyers advising corporate investors will need to examine the context for the investment and assess and advise on the risks of potential human rights violations and the means to avoid and if necessary address adverse impacts.

The types of issues which may arise in the context of large-scale land acquisition include adverse impacts on the food security and livelihoods of those whose customary rights are not respected, including those farming the land, or using the land seasonally for grazing or forage or for access to water or fishing. The right to housing under Article 11(1) ICESCR also includes protection from forced eviction as confirmed by the CESCR in 1997 in its General Comment No 7 (considered further below). The right to property may also be engaged, possibly in conjunction with the rights of indigenous peoples to communal tenure of ancestral land, (IACtHR, 2005). The rights of indigenous peoples over their ancestral land, and in particular the right of FPIC, may be impacted and may affect the scope of other rights, including the right to property.[29]

The right to life may be engaged where impacts on conditions of life are such as to constitute a violation, for example where the State has not adopted the necessary positive measures which could reasonably be expected in order to prevent or avoid risking the right to life.[30]

---

[29] For example, in a case brought against a State by members of the Sawhoyamaxa indigenous community for failure to guarantee the right to property over ancestral lands, the Inter-American Court of Human Rights (IACtHR) ruled that possession is not a requisite for the existence of indigenous land restitution rights. The State's failure had deprived the community concerned not only of the material possession of their lands but also of the fundamental basis to develop their culture and economic survival (IACtHR, 2006).

[30] This was also an issue in the Sawhoyamaxa case, in relation to a lack of effective access to health care in the context of the dispute over land (IACtHR, 2006, paras 150-178, pp.80-87).

Although it is the State which is liable for failing to take positive measures, in circumstances where a business has contributed to the situation through purchase of disputed land, the UNGP, read in the light of the VGGT and the CFS-RAI will be relevant. Lawyers advising clients in such a situation should address these risks, or potential risks, in their advice, bearing in mind the red flags laid down in TG No. 7 (FAO, 2016) and the direction in the OECD/FAO Guidance that higher risk areas should be subject to enhanced due diligence (OECD/FAO, 2016).

There may also be potential human rights issues relating to the position of those who become contract farmers or outgrowers following the acquisition of land for commercial investment, if they become indebted through the need to take out unsustainable loans. The comprehensive Legal Guide on Contract Farming is aligned with the CFS-RAI and is relevant in this context.

The Guide notes that:

> From a human rights-based perspective, there are several principles that should be incorporated into the negotiation and implementation of agricultural production contracts. Participation, accountability, empowerment, non-discrimination, transparency, human dignity and the rule of law are some of the principles that business models such as contract farming should encompass (UNIDROIT, IFAD and FAO, 2015).[31]

The adverse impacts of unsustainable debt on peasant farmers generally are well documented, leading in some cases to suicide (HRC, 2012). In these circumstances, it is important to monitor the arrangements for contract farming and outgrowing to ensure that these will not entail the need to take on unsustainable loans or debts or exacerbate existing issues with debt-bondage or extremely low agricultural wages. Lawyers should take account of these factors as highlighted in the impact assessment when advising on or drafting agreements with those taking on such roles, bearing in mind their rights under human rights treaties including the ICESCR.

Labour rights are also highly relevant in this context, particularly where displaced people, including children, may take on paid labour in order to compensate for the loss of land or other resources on which their livelihood was previously based. Labour rights are protected under conventions of the ILO, including international prohibitions on child labour.[32] International labour standards should be considered together with relevant international human rights law rights and principles, including the right to form and join trade unions (ICESCR, Article 8), the rights of the child under the CRC, the right to just and favourable conditions of work, including fair wages (ICESCR, Article 7), and the principles of non-discrimination and equality as laid down in the ICESCR, CEDAW, CERD and CRDP.

FAO has published an assessment, including legal guidance, on international labour standards that are relevant to the agriculture, forestry and fisheries sectors (FAO, 2016(c)). As indicated in FAO guidance:

> In terms of labour standards, the agriculture sector tends to be under-regulated either as a result of its tacit or express exclusion from pertinent laws or the failure of such laws to address the particular circumstances of agricultural workers (p.2).[33]

---

[31] The International Institute for the Unification of Private Law (UNIDROIT), in collaboration with FAO and IFAD, is preparing a legal guide on agricultural land investment contracts for use by counsel working on the leasing of agricultural land, whether from States, customary authorities or private parties. See https://www.unidroit.org/work-in-progress/agricultural-land-investment.

[32] These include ILO Convention No. 182 on the worst forms of child labour, 1999; ILO Convention No. 138 on the minimum age for admission to employment and work and ILO Convention No. 10 - Minimum Age (Agriculture), 1921.

[33] The Assessment cites *Promotion of Rural Employment for Poverty Reduction*, International Labour Conference, 97th session, report IV, ILO, 2008 Geneva.

DUE DILIGENCE, TENURE AND AGRICULTURAL INVESTMENT

A guide on the dual responsibilities of private sector lawyers in advising on the acquisition of land and natural resources

This assessment also highlights the extent to which such standards fail to take account of the position of groups such as pastoralists, fishers and forest dependent peoples who may suffer from marginalization. However, many standards will be relevant, including the ILO's four fundamental principles and rights at work which are considered to be applicable to all forms of work in agriculture (FAO, 2016(c)).[34]

Labour standards are addressed in the VGGT, the SSF Guidelines, the CFS-RAI and the Voluntary Guidelines to Support the Progressive Realization of the Right to Adequate Food in the Context of National Food Security (Guideline 8A) among other soft law instruments.

It is particularly important therefore, that in the context of the acquisition of land and other natural resources for the purposes of agricultural investment, regard is had to international labour standards that are relevant to the impact of the investment on tenure right holders and other affected communities, including employment or contractual arrangements that the investor intends to enter into as a result of the investment (FAO, 2016(c)). Lawyers advising on such investments should ensure that these standards are included in advice relating to due diligence as set out below.

The Special Rapporteur on the Right to Food has warned states that they act in violation of the human right to food if: 'by leasing or selling land to investors (domestic or foreign), they deprive local populations of access to the productive resources indispensable to their livelihoods, or if they negotiate investment agreements without ensuring food security for their populations' (HRC, 2009).

Impacts on women may be particularly severe, as recognised by the CESCR (see above). CEDAW addresses the particular problems faced by rural women and requires States to ensure rural women a range of rights including the right to have equal treatment in land and agrarian reform as well as in land resettlement schemes (Article 14 CEDAW).

There may also be issues of harassment and forced eviction, discussed below, as well as interference with freedom of association and freedom of expression.

The need to avoid and address adverse impacts is also relevant to fisheries and forests which are covered by the VGGT including the award of fishing licenses in relation to fisheries which are important for those with customary rights, or fished by SSF communities, and the grant of logging concessions for forestry where this impacts on those with customary rights to forest resources, including indigenous peoples. If such licenses put the State concerned in breach of its international human rights obligations, this also has implications for businesses to whom those licenses are awarded, within the framework set out in the UNGP, VGGT and CFS-RAI.

The UNGP require businesses to take into account the severity of likely impacts in designing the measures which will ensure that human rights are respected. In this area, the vulnerability of the communities likely to be affected and the gravity of the impacts likely to be caused, including increases in poverty and food insecurity which may pose a threat to life and health, all indicate that adverse impacts will be at the severe end of the scale. The commentary to UNGP 14 states that 'severity of impacts will be judged by their scale, scope and irremediable character' (see also IBA, 2016(a)). This should be assessed on an ongoing basis both by reference to specific projects and in order to refine general methodology and effective risk assessment (IBA, 2016(a)).

---

[34] The Assessment cites the ILO, *Declaration on Fundamental Principles and Rights at Work and its Follow-up*, 1998. A comprehensive outline of the international labour standards applicable to work in the agriculture, forestry, fisheries and aquaculture sectors is set out in Annex 1 to FAO, 2016(c), pp.18-24.

Businesses and their advisors should be sensitive to the implications of State reform to land registration or titling, since land titling 'can give small-scale food producers more security over their land, but it can also help governments expropriate land for large-scale land acquisitions' (ActionAid, 2015).[35]

3.1.1 Avoid and address

The central guiding principle of the UNGP is that businesses should avoid infringing the human rights of others and address adverse human rights impacts with which they are involved (UNGP 11). The OHCHR Interpretive Guide explains avoidance in this context as meaning that 'enterprises can go about their activities, within the law, so long as they do not cause harm to individuals' human rights in the process' but that:

> ...If an enterprise evicts a community without due process, consultation and compensation, it will infringe the right to adequate housing (OHCHR, 2012).

In the context of tenure rights and associated human rights, avoidance must entail conducting due diligence as this will enable the business to assess the risks of impacts which it must avoid. This is reinforced by the duty under the CFS-RAI to act with due diligence to avoid infringing human rights. The conduct of due diligence will in this way also enable businesses to address the risks of infringement by taking preventive action as discussed below. In their advice to clients and their conduct of negotiations, drafting agreements and monitoring of projects, law firms should focus, on an ongoing basis, on alerting the client to the legal implications of potential negative impacts and supporting the client to avoid and address these. Particular attention should be paid to marginalised and vulnerable groups which may be affected by the actions of the client in the context of agricultural investment and in circumstances where recognition or protection of these rights under national law may be incomplete or weak.

Lawyers should advise clients as to the factors which international technical guidance has identified as indicating that an investment may pose risks in terms of infringements of human rights and tenure rights. This falls within the avoidance duty placed on both the client and their legal advisors under the UNGP. In the context of the preliminary assessment phase for responsible investment in land, FAO technical guidance for investors highlights risk factors which indicate that an investment is high risk or medium risk (FAO, 2016).

High risk factors include the following: the project design requires the large-scale transfer of land rights from local people, possibly resulting in many people being involuntarily resettled; indigenous communities have not given their FPIC to the investment; the site has forests or is in an area of high conservation value that is likely to be destroyed or harmed by the project; or that, in weak land governance settings, the operator/direct investor has not and will not carry out mapping, impact assessment or an inclusive community consultation process, among other factors (FAO, 2016).

Medium risk factors include the following: human rights violations have been reported in the area, indigenous peoples live near the site, the communal land targeted by the investor is wrongly categorized as unused or uninhabited or that an independent environmental and social impact assessment (ESIA) has not been completed, among others (FAO, 2016).

---

[35] The report refers to World Bank research of this issue, which recognized that individual titling can weaken or leave out communal, secondary or women's rights.

DUE DILIGENCE, TENURE AND AGRICULTURAL INVESTMENT

A guide on the dual responsibilities of private sector lawyers in advising on the acquisition of land and natural resources

Technical guidance for investors advises that where high risk factors are identified, the responsible investor should not proceed with the investment and where medium risk factors are identified, the investor should proceed with caution, seek to mitigate the risks, and decide not to proceed if the risks cannot be addressed (FAO, 2016).

Avoidance in this context would preclude action which circumvents national legal protection of tenure rights and access to land for small-scale rural producers or others who need access to the land. For example, circumventing national rules on the concentration of land reserved for small-scale producers by means of fragmented purchases using shell companies, in order to avoid restrictions on purchase of such land from smallholders, would almost certainly infringe the requirement to avoid adverse impacts.

3.1.2 Integrated and comprehensive impact assessment

It is important that those advising on human rights due diligence in the context of investment take account of the range of requirements for consultation and impact assessment under international and national frameworks. In 2014, France's Technical Committee on Land and Development published a comprehensive operational guide to due diligence of agribusiness projects that affect land and property rights (Technical Committee, 2014). The operational guide refers to a number of relevant international standards that are relevant to the implementation of the VGGT at country level.

The IFC has adopted a range of environmental and social performance standards which are relevant to agricultural investment and the acquisition of land and natural resources (IFC, 2012). As part of its Sustainability Framework, the IFC has adopted Performance Standard 5 (PS5) on Land Acquisition and Involuntary Resettlement[36] and Performance Standard 7 on Indigenous Peoples (PS7).[37] IFC Performance Standard 1 establishes the importance of: (i) integrated assessment to identify the environmental and social impacts, risks, and opportunities; (ii) effective community engagement through disclosure of project-related information and consultation with local communities; and (iii) the client's management of environmental and social performance throughout the life of the project.

The Performance Standards underpin the IFC's social and due diligence process in respect of IFC clients and provide guidance on the management of environmental and social risks. They can also be considered more widely as representing international good practice in due diligence (Technical Committee, 2014).

A number of international organisations and international private sector organisations have also adopted specific standards in this area which may also be relevant to the project concerned, depending on the sector.[38]

In order to ensure that human rights are respected in line with the UNGP and the VGGT, as well as relevant human rights laws, there should be coherence between environmental and social impact assessment and consultation and the specific focus of human rights due diligence. The impact assessment should include consideration of the full range of human rights:

---

[36] PS 5 was adopted on January 1, 2012. See also IFC Guidance Note 5 on Land Acquisition and Involuntary Resettlement also adopted 1 January 2012 (https://www.ifc.org/wps/wcm/connect/topics_ext_content/ifc_external_corporate_site/sustainability-at-ifc/policies-standards/performance-standards/ps5).

[37] See the comparative analysis in Windfuhr 2017. Publikationen/ANALYSE/Analyse__Safeguarding_Human_Rights_in_Land_Related_Investments_bf.pdf.

[38] These include the World Commission on Dams (WCD), the Extractive Industries Review (EIR), the Forest Stewardship Council (FSC), the Roundtable on Sustainable Palm Oil (RSPO), the Round Table on Responsible Soy Association (RTRS) and the Roundtable on Sustainable Biomaterials (RSB), (FAO, 2014(a), p.7).

> Given that all human rights are universal, indivisible, interdependent and interrelated, the governance of tenure of land, fisheries and forests should not only take into account rights that are directly linked to access and use of land, fisheries and forests, but also all civil, political, economic, social and cultural rights (VGGT).[39]

It follows that in order to prevent or mitigate impacts on human rights, the full range of human rights relevant to the specific investment and its potential impacts should also be addressed in legal advice. UNGP 19 directs that:

> In order to prevent and mitigate adverse human rights impacts, business enterprises should integrate the findings from their impact assessments across relevant internal functions and processes, and take appropriate action…[which]…will vary according to:
>
> 1. Whether the business enterprise causes or contributes to an adverse impact, or whether it is involved solely because the impact is directly linked to its operations, products or services by a business relationship;
> 2. The extent of its leverage in addressing the adverse impact.

Any deliberate omission of relevant areas of advice, such as full coverage of relevant human rights, would not appear to constitute 'appropriate action' particularly where this increases the prospect that human rights will not be respected as a consequence of the actions of the client. Lawyers will wish to use the leverage that they have, particularly where there are risks of serious violations of human rights, to avoid and address these risks as discussed in Section 2.

Lawyers advising their clients will also wish to bear in mind the VGGT implementing principles including those relating to non-discrimination and gender (VGGT). In respecting human rights in the way that they provide their legal services, lawyers should consider their own obligations not to discriminate, for example by omitting to address issues of potential discrimination and breaches of the equality principle in the advice that they give and in the way that they support the operational side of due diligence, including supporting consultation with stakeholders.

Box 3.2 Domestic and foreign investment

There may be differences between due diligence requirements placed on foreign investors and those required of domestic investors as highlighted by FAO in 2015:

> …domestic investors are often not registered and/or do not face the same due diligence process regarding business plans as foreign investors face, making it much more difficult to safeguard tenure rights, monitor investments and direct them towards development objectives (FAO, TG No. 4).

Bearing in mind the direction in the UNGP to avoid infringing human rights and prevent adverse impacts, private sector lawyers should ensure that due diligence is conducted consistent with VGGT and UNGP standards, whether the investment is made by a foreign or, domestic investor or under a joint venture between the two. Legal advisors will wish to consider carefully whether any joint venture with domestic investors is likely to circumvent protections afforded to tenure and human rights in relation to foreign investment. Legal advisors should alert clients to this risk in advising on the project as part of the law firm's own avoidance of human rights breaches or adverse impacts if they take the view that these risks are higher for domestic investment.

../cont.

---

[39] See also FAO, 2015, p.59.

A guide on the dual responsibilities of private sector lawyers in advising on the acquisition of land and natural resources

---

Box 3.2 Domestic and foreign investment (cont.)

Legal advisors should alert clients to this risk in advising on the project as part of the law firm's own avoidance of human rights breaches or adverse impacts if they take the view that these risks are higher for domestic investment.

Investment agreements form an important part of the legal context for large-scale land acquisitions. A full analysis of the implications of international investment law for these transactions is beyond the scope of this guide. However a number of key issues which bear on the due diligence of businesses and their legal advisors can be highlighted, as outlined below.

The legal implications of the system of national governance of tenure for investor/State disputes will depend on the terms of the relevant agreement and the facts of the case. However, the conduct of the investor in relation to the protection of legitimate tenure rights may come under scrutiny, particularly where the transaction is contested on the grounds that these rights have been breached or disregarded.

In relation to investment agreements, there is concern that these could undermine governments' attempts to regulate in the public interest including by strengthening local resources rights or that stabilisation clauses will make it difficult for governments to introduce regulatory reform over the period of the contract (Cotula and Berger, 2017).

The issue of legitimate expectation may arise in the context of determining whether the fair and equitable treatment standard has been, or is likely to be, breached (Cotula, 2016). Commentators have debated whether an investor's expectation can be 'legitimate' in circumstances where the expectation is that a land related acquisition will be concluded without reference to, or respect for, the legitimate tenure rights addressed in the VGGT and without adequate due diligence, as required under the UNGP and VGGT. Even where official, or purportedly official, assurances have been given to that effect, the question arises as to whether conduct in breach of international standards, such as consultation, FPIC or protection from forced eviction, can be the subject of legitimate expectation.

Legal advisors will wish to advise their clients as to the risks arising from transactions which do not comply with VGGT and/or CFS-RAI standards, both reputational and in terms of the risk of an adverse outcome in potential investor state arbitration claims. If local opposition to an investment which has been initiated in breach of the international standards for consultation and transparency results in delay for example, it is questionable that such an obstruction can constitute a breach of legitimate expectation on the part of the investor.[40]

The rest of this Section addresses specific elements of due diligence by which law firms can assist their clients to 'know and show' that they are identifying, preventing, mitigating and accounting for adverse human rights impacts (UNGP, 2011) and also ensure that they meet this obligation in their own right, whilst respecting professional obligations to the client.

---

[40] See discussion in Cotula, 2017(b), p.262-264.

3.2 STAGES OF THE DUE DILIGENCE PROCESS

The stages of due diligence include:

- adopting and integrating into existing systems a policy on human rights due diligence (see Section 2, the subsequent stages set out below are addressed in this Section);

- assessing actual and potential impacts on human rights and tenure rights by:

  — mapping impacts through conducting surveys of potential areas of investment/land acquisition, including baseline data on those with tenure rights and user rights, or otherwise likely to be impacted by the project;

  — carrying out a regulatory review of relevant national laws governing tenure and the rights of those likely to be affected, including vulnerable groups, indigenous peoples and vulnerable individuals;

  — conducting consultation and ensuring participation of all potentially affected stakeholders;

- integrating the findings from the survey, consultation and proactive impact assessment into subsequent responsive action, including in the preparation of contracts and agreements for approval by the relevant authorities and parties to the agreements and taking action to prevent or mitigate any breaches/potential breaches of human rights and associated tenure rights;

- tracking and monitoring impacts on human rights and tenure rights;

- communicating and reporting on how those impacts are being addressed ; and

- establishing and operating appropriate grievance mechanisms.

See UNGP, 2011, UNGP 17-21; FAO, 2015; FAO, 2014; Section 3 of the FAO/OECD Guidance: Five-step framework for risk-based due diligence along agricultural supply chains, IBA, 2016.

3.2.1 Mapping

As indicated by the IBA:

> Human rights due diligence means that a business should map its human rights risks by severity and likelihood. Through its own activities and its business relationships, a business can impact the rights of various different stakeholders, such as…local communities around its operations. Some of those stakeholders may belong to potentially marginalised or vulnerable groups, who may sometimes be the least visible or vocal in a society, and as a result, could experience more severe negative impacts (IBA, 2016(a)).

DUE DILIGENCE, TENURE AND AGRICULTURAL INVESTMENT

A guide on the dual responsibilities of private sector lawyers in advising on the acquisition of land and natural resources

The type of mapping indicated by the IBA should include, in this context, advising and assisting clients on how to map human rights or tenure rights risks with reference to particular projects, and:

- ensuring that clients are aware of, and can address, difficulties in identifying vulnerable groups and individuals and that clients consider potential impacts on such groups and individuals by reference to the applicable international legal frameworks, including, but not limited to, the ICESCR, the ICCPR, CEDAW, the CRC, UNDRIP and CERD. Vulnerable individuals, groups and communities are those that face a particular risk of being exposed to discrimination and other adverse human rights impacts. People who are disadvantaged, marginalised or excluded from society are often particularly vulnerable (OHCHR, 2012);

- ensuring that the firm advises on the basis of the latest and best available evidence and addresses specific key risks including the risk of dispossession, forced eviction, loss of livelihood, food insecurity and harassment;

- ensuring that both the client and their legal advisors have regard to UNGP 23(c) (UNGP, 2011), which provides that businesses should treat 'the risk of causing or contributing to gross human rights abuses as a legal compliance issue wherever they operate'. Particular attention should be given to any operation on or near conflict zones or in circumstances where there is risk of mass eviction of a minority group, or other gross human rights violation; and

- ensuring that all lawyers involved in advising on the project have sufficient expertise to advise on these issues including by undertaking training, seeking outside expertise where needed, and building up best practice based on experience in areas such as the conduct of public consultations, whilst protecting confidential information as appropriate.

The assessment of the social and economic position of stakeholders should be accompanied by a regulatory review of the protection afforded to tenure rights and of the operational status of any national legal protection, taking into account any barriers to the registration of rights or the enforcement of protections. Technical guidance published by FAO highlights the difficulties associated with weak governance of rights to the commons, both because of a lack of legal recognition of customary rights and because of a lack of capacity among communities to exercise and protect their rights (FAO, 2016(a)). Due diligence entails acting so as to have regard to this context so that rights which may be poorly recognised and or enforced are not disregarded.

Technical Guidance on FPIC advises businesses to:

> Engage a consultant or lawyer to carry out a thorough review of existing national legal, institutional and policy frameworks. Ideally, the consultant should employ innovative and interdisciplinary investigation methods, as well as a participatory and collaborative approach throughout the research process. (FAO, 2014(a)).

CFS-RAI Principle 10 indicates the importance of defining baseline data and indicators by which to monitor and measure impacts and by regularly assessing changes and communicating results (FAO, 2014).

It is important for clients and their advisors to be sensitive to the situation on the ground as well as to the national legal and policy framework. As indicated in technical guidance, boundaries may appear unclear or vague to outsiders whereas the rights holders themselves may be well aware of their community boundaries and members (FAO, 2016(a)). This indicates the need for thorough on the ground analysis and direct consultation with tenure rights holders. Technical guidance on the commons indicates the need to study the official land register as well as to conduct an on-site investigation 'in order to identify rights not disclosed in government records' (FAO, 2016(a)).

There should be an *ex ante* analysis of the tenure status of the farms and territories concerned which identifies all right-holders, including those with customary grazing and water rights, as well as sites of cultural value and areas which provide natural services such as watershed protection, prior to any transaction (FAO 2014(a)). This identification of right-holders should be an open process and should be published or made available to the community concerned. One guide to due diligence in this sector states that:

> All projects should be preceded by a feasibility study, which should routinely be accompanied by an environmental and social impact assessment (ESIA) (Technical Committee, 2014).

This report then notes that this is not always done, particularly in relation to social impacts, and that sometimes the project is finalized before an ESIA has been produced.

The assessment should consider whether, in the light of the regulatory review, there are adequate provisions for transparency, stakeholder involvement and accountability in the agricultural investment project design, approval, monitoring and evaluation processes. Lawyers should be alert to the risk that only a small proportion of local rights are formally recognised under national law leading to: '…the erroneous assumption that land is free of rights, when it is in fact subject to a wide range of informal rights that are not recognised by the State but which reflect well-established, locally recognised regulatory systems…' (Technical Committee, 2014).

3.2.2 Consultation and participation

Assessing human rights impacts means seeking to take into account the perspective of potentially affected stakeholders wherever possible, through meaningful engagement with them or their representatives. Understanding their perspective is essential in order to accurately assess the severity and probability of impacts on them (IBA, 2016(a)).

The VGGT are to be implemented on the basis of a robust approach to consultation as Principle 3B.6 makes clear:

> …engaging with and seeking the support of those who, having legitimate tenure rights, could be affected by decisions, prior to decisions being taken, and responding to their contributions; taking into consideration existing power imbalances between different parties and ensuring active, free, effective, meaningful and informed participation of individuals and groups in associated decision-making processes…

The requirement for meaningful consultation and participation as part of human rights due diligence is also a robust one, as indicated in international human rights jurisprudence and in guidance issued by international bodies, including FAO and international courts and tribunals. As emphasised by the African Commission on Human and Peoples Rights in the *Enderois case*, participation should be meaningful and effective to comply with human rights standards.[41] Communities should not simply be presented with a fait accompli. In the case of *Sarayaku v*

---

[41] The Commission referred to Article 2(3) of the UN Declaration on Development, which provides that the right to development includes "active, free and meaningful participation in development", see discussion at para. 36.

DUE DILIGENCE, TENURE AND AGRICULTURAL INVESTMENT

A guide on the dual responsibilities of private sector lawyers in advising on the acquisition of land and natural resources

Ecuador, the IACtHR looked at cases decided in the Americas and elsewhere and concluded that the obligation to consult: 'in addition to being a treaty-based provision, is also a general principle of international law'.

The Court also observed that:

> ...the obligation of States to carry out special and differentiated consultation processes when certain interests of indigenous peoples and communities are about to be affected is an obligation that has been clearly recognized. Such processes must respect the particular consultation system of each people or community, so that it can be understood as an appropriate and effective interaction with State authorities, political and social actors and interested third parties.

In *Saramaka People v Suriname*, the IACtHR held that:

> ...in order to guarantee that restrictions to the property rights of the members of the Saramaka people by the issuance of concessions within their territory does not amount to a denial of their survival as a tribal people, the State must ...ensure the effective participation of the members of the Saramaka people, in conformity with their customs and traditions, regarding any development, investment, exploration or extraction plan ...

The Court noted that those safeguards were consistent with the observations of the UN Human Rights Committee, the text of several international instruments, and the practice in several States parties to the American Convention on Human Rights. The Court then went on to specify that:

> These consultations must be in good faith, through culturally appropriate procedures and with the objective of reaching an agreement... Early notice provides time for internal discussion within communities and for proper feedback to the State. Finally, consultation should take account of the Saramaka people's traditional methods of decision-making ...

Under the VGGT, States are required to ensure that transfers of rights do not have any undesirable impacts on local communities and to ensure the fair and equitable involvement of legitimate community bodies in the process (FAO, 2016(a)). The VGGT call for States to ensure that investments are consistent with the principles of consultation and participation. These are core requirements for any responsible agricultural investment (FAO, 2015). Where proposed investments affect indigenous peoples, consultations should aim to obtain their FPIC (VGGT), discussed below.

Where consultation and participation are conditions for investment, a failure to conduct consultation and participation in good faith would undermine the basis for the investment. Lawyers will wish to advise on the duty of good faith in relation to consultation and participation, having regard to the VGGT, UNDRIP and international human rights instruments and jurisprudence, including the requirement that participation be meaningful (capable of affecting the outcome). Guidance on consultation, participation and negotiations with affected communities and individuals emphasises the importance of early consultation and of planning the consultation, participation and negotiation process in a community engagement plan that the community has agreed to at the outset (FAO, 2016).

Good faith consultations go well beyond a right to be informed, to an openness on the part of the investor to engaging with community concerns and modifying the proposal accordingly, bearing in mind the requirement to prevent or mitigate adverse human rights impacts in UNGP 13 and Principle 3B.6 of the VGGT. Consultation should be conducted in an effective way:

> Engagement can only be effective if it takes place at the right point in the decision-making process: before and during the contract negotiations and throughout the life of the investment project. The

common practice of holding a public hearing only at the end of a planning and negotiation process is inefficient as it can easily result in calls for a complete re-planning to take stakeholders' thoughts into account (FAO, 2015).

As to the scope of consultation, FAO technical guide for investment promotion agencies outlines the information which should, depending on the stage and type of investment, be provided prior to the investment approval being made:

> ...the nature, size and duration of the investment; the objective of the investment; the locations/ areas that will be affected by the investment, including indirectly; a preliminary assessment of the possible impacts, including risks and benefits; procedures and timeframe for developing the investment; government and investment personnel serving as focal points with communities (FAO, 2015).

Non-State actors, as well as States, should endeavour to prevent corruption with respect to tenure systems of indigenous peoples and others with customary rights, by ensuring consultation, participation and empowerment (VGGT). The need to prevent corruption will engage a level of vigilance derived from UNCAC as well as the VGGT.

Guidance on what constitutes participatory EIA in relation to FPIC has been provided by FAO (FAO, 2014(a)). Lawyers advising investors should ensure that the business entity provides appropriate information about itself and the project (FAO, 2014(a)), including as to compensation and mitigation measures it proposes to take.

Technical guidance has also emphasised the importance of independent advice for communities:

> Communities must be free to choose their own independent advisers separate from, and/or in addition to, risk assessors or specialists recommended or commissioned by the government or investor. The results of these impact assessments must be publicly disclosed and considered in the contract negotiations in a transparent way (FAO, 2016(a)).

Lawyers advising on the scope of the FPIC standard under international law should also take into account the extent to which it is increasingly emerging as best practice. Technical guidance indicates that many private companies apply the FPIC standard more widely in relation to the sourcing of products and land transactions (FAO, 2015).

Box 3.3 Free, prior and informed consent

The VGGT underline the importance of recognising the tenure systems of indigenous peoples and other communities with customary tenure systems (FAO, 2012, VGGT). VGGT paragraph 9.9 calls on states and other parties to hold good faith consultations with indigenous peoples before initiating any project, or before adopting and implementing legislative or administrative measures affecting the resources for which the communities hold rights. Such projects should be based on an effective and meaningful consultation with indigenous peoples, through their own representative institutions in order to obtain their FPIC under UNDRIP (UNGA, 2008) and with due regard for particular positions and understandings of individual States. VGGT paragraph 9.9 also confirms that:

> The principles of consultation and participation, as set out in paragraph 3B.6, should be applied in the case of other communities described in this section.

In relation to FPIC, the right is: 'to effectively determine the outcome of decision-making that affects them, not merely a right to be involved in such processes' (FAO, 2014(a)).

DUE DILIGENCE, TENURE AND AGRICULTURAL INVESTMENT

A guide on the dual responsibilities of private sector lawyers in advising on the acquisition of land and natural resources

As indicated in technical guidance:

> Many private companies have ...declared that they will institute a policy of obtaining FPIC in all sourcing of products and in their own land transactions. Many private certification schemes require adherence to FPIC for all investors seeking certification (FAO, 2015).

> Jurisprudential interpretation by human rights bodies and the increasing inclusion of FPIC as a right of indigenous peoples and other local communities in the operational policies of international financial institutions and other non-State entities support this expanded reach of the right to FPIC. It can therefore be argued that *all communities should have a meaningful role in making decisions about development projects that, directly, affect them, including the ability to decide not to proceed if they are not in favour of an investment* (FAO, 2015) (emphasis added).

Lawyers should advise their clients on the evolving best practice in relation to this extended application of FPIC, as operating a narrow approach may expose the client to reputational risk. This important area could be addressed in training, see Section 2.3.3 above.

The FPIC standard applies to the zoning and sale of resource concessions, land acquisition, leasing of land, and national plans for resource development or extraction (FAO, 2014(a) and FAO, 2016(a)). Where investments establish arrangements such as outgrowing and contract farming, the arrangements for these, including wage rates and the likelihood that the farmers concerned will need to take out loans, should be specific and guaranteed so that consent based on those arrangements is informed.

Annex B to the OECD/FAO Guidance addresses the situation where FPIC is not required under national law:

> In countries where FPIC is not mandated, enterprises should consider local expectations, the risks posed to indigenous peoples and to the operations as a result of local opposition. They should pursue an engagement strategy that meets the legitimate expectations of indigenous peoples to the extent that they do not violate domestic law.[42]

Technical guidance also states that where Indigenous communities have not given their FPIC, this constitutes a high risk factor indicating that the investment should not be proceeded with (FAO, 2016).

3.2.3 Impact assessment based on proactive approach

UNGP17 states that the human rights due diligence process should include:

> Assessing actual and potential human rights impacts, integrating and acting upon the findings, tracking responses, and communicating how impacts are addressed.

The OHCHR Guide to the UNGP advises the process should begin as early as possible (OHCHR, 2012).

Lawyers can advise and assist their clients by taking a proactive approach to due diligence and seeking the information which is essential for effective consultation and impact assessment, not only in cases where FPIC applies but more generally. In the context of issuing the OECD/FAO Guidance, the OECD Council has described due diligence generally as:

> ...an on-going, proactive and reactive process through which enterprises can ensure that they observe government-backed standards for responsible agricultural supply chains related to human

---

[42] See also OECD/FAO, 2016 p. 81 (action where consent is not forthcoming).

rights…tenure rights…and the use of natural resources…(Recommendations of the OECD Council on the OECD/FAO Guidance for Responsible Agricultural Supply Chains, Preamble) (emphasis added).

The identification of all legitimate tenure rights and their holders in the area covered by the planned investment should be addressed in the impact assessment which should then:

…analyse the potential positive and negative impacts that the investment may have on these rights and right holders. The objective is to avoid any significant negative impacts by identifying tenure solutions and arrangements for the investor that do not harm existing right holders (FAO, 2015).

Clients and their legal advisors should also consider the gender impact of agreements. FAO technical guidance states:

…contracts are often made with men, and women may lose rights to use land for food production when a male head of household accepts a contract for commercial crop production. These situations can be avoided by engaging both women and men landowners and users in negotiations of investment models (FAO, 2015).

Given that the responsibility of businesses to respect human rights entails, inter alia, seeking: 'to prevent or mitigate adverse human rights impacts that are directly linked to their operations, products or services by their business relationships, even if they have not contributed to those impacts' (UNGP 13(b)), lawyers advising investors will wish to adopt a proactive approach to ensuring that full information is available on the communities and right holders who may be affected by an investment or acquisition.

In the context of respecting the principle of FPIC, technical guidance on FPIC advises that companies (and this would imply by extension their legal advisors) should check that the government concerned has supplied the required information about the legal status of communities, their rights, the legal status of the land and the legal implications of the proposed land use change for those rights (FAO, 2014(a)).

Lawyers will need to advise their clients that, while national law may not robustly underpin the need to consult local communities, the internationally recognised human rights which clients should respect under the UNGP cannot be respected in the absence of such consultation:

While some laws require governments or investors to consult local communities before concluding a land concession or lease… others do not, and implementation has often fallen short of expectations (Cotula, 2016).

Technical guidance for investors advises that projects should be designed or modified, if necessary, to avoid causing harm and indicates measures which may achieve this, including ensuring that community members continue to have secure access to some land for subsistence farming and other livelihood activities (FAO, 2016). Lawyers can advise on the legal implications of potential harms and the legal framework which supports such mitigation within the scope of the responsibility to respect human rights and avoid and address adverse impacts under the UNGP (see above). The technical guidance also advises that, where harms cannot be avoided, the investment should not continue (FAO, 2016). This proactive approach can be seen as reflected in the 'wise counsellor' role described in IBA guidance as discussed in Section 2.

The professional duty of lawyers to avoid conflicts of interest may affect the ways in which the VGGT are applied. For example, in carrying out consultations with affected communities in the context of proposed investment projects (VGGT section 12), lawyers need to exercise due diligence to avoid conflicts of interest that could occur when private investors pay the costs of the communities' legal counsel (FAO, 2016(b)).

DUE DILIGENCE, TENURE AND AGRICULTURAL INVESTMENT

A guide on the dual responsibilities of private sector lawyers in advising on the acquisition of land and natural resources

No forcible evictions

One area where lawyers should be particularly vigilant and proactive in advising clients relates to the risk of forced evictions. The impacts of dispossession are highlighted in the VGGT, which note that:

> People can be condemned to a life of hunger and poverty if they lose their tenure rights to their homes, land, fisheries and forests and their livelihoods because of corrupt tenure practices or if implementing agencies fail to protect their tenure rights. People may even lose their lives when weak tenure governance leads to violent conflict (VGGT).

This indicates that loss of tenure rights is likely to involve a high risk of human rights violations. The specific issue of forced eviction is then addressed a number of times:

> All forms of tenure should provide all persons with a degree of tenure security which guarantees legal protection against forced evictions that are inconsistent with States' existing obligations under national and international law, and against harassment and other threats (VGGT).

In its General Comment on forced evictions, the CESCR defines forced evictions as:

> …the permanent or temporary removal against their will of individuals, families and/or communities from the homes and/or land which they occupy, without the provision of, and access to, appropriate forms of legal or other protection. The prohibition on forced evictions does not, however, apply to evictions carried out by force in accordance with the law and in conformity with the provisions of the International Covenants on Human Rights (CESCR, 1997).

The General Comment notes that forced evictions frequently violate other human rights, including civil and political rights, and that evictions may be carried out in connection with conflict over land rights, development and infrastructure projects and the clearing of land for agricultural purposes (CESCR, 1997).[43]

The VGGT state that, where it is not possible to provide legal recognition of tenure rights, States should prevent forced evictions inconsistent with obligations under national or international law (VGGT). States should also expropriate only where rights to land, fisheries or forests are required for a public purpose and the concept of public purpose should be clearly defined in law, in order to allow for judicial review. (VGGT).[44] This emphasis on legal accountability places a particular onus on lawyers advising investors to have regard to the risks arising from lack of adequate legal protection against forced evictions in national law, since this is a matter on which risk management is directly dependent on legal advice.

Technical guidance for investors also indicates that all forced evictions should be avoided, even where compensation is to be provided (FAO, 2016). This indicates that forced evictions should be prevented where this is inconsistent with international human rights law and/or national constitutional law. Risks include potential infringements of the prohibition of discrimination on grounds of ethnicity, gender or other status. This is clearly an area where lawyers will need to scrutinise very carefully any proposed forced evictions to which the actions of their clients are linked or to which their actions have contributed. The law firm may wish to highlight this as a 'red flag' or high risk area which it will monitor closely in relation to its own human rights policy and professional conduct, and in the light of a commitment to withdraw if asked to facilitate violations of human rights protection measures.

---

[43] See also the Basic principles and guidelines on development-based evictions and displacement (HRC, 2007), Annex 1 of the report of the Special Rapporteur on adequate housing as a component of the right to an adequate standard of living, A/HRC/4/18.

[44] See also OECD/FAO, 2016, the Model Enterprise Policy, section 6 at p.28: 'We are aware that, subject to their national law and legislation and in accordance with national context, states should expropriate only where the rights at issue are required for a public purpose and should ensure a prompt, adequate and effective compensation.'

FAO has issued guidance which recommends that State authorities monitor any increases in evictions and increases in landlessness after an investment has been agreed, to be included among the indicators to be used for measuring the impact of investment projects on local people's tenure rights (FAO, 2015). Lawyers will wish to ensure that, in relation to individual projects on which they are advising, these impacts are monitored and addressed within the framework of international and national human rights laws and that this forms part of the ongoing tracking provided for in UNGP Principle 20, considered further below.

3.3 DRAFTING CONTRACTS

The UNGP, in Appendix D, address contractual drafting and negotiations through the Principles for Responsible Contracts (UNGP Contract Principles). The broader relevance of these Principles is highlighted in IBA, 2016(a):

> While the Contract Principles were intended to apply only to State-investor negotiations, their overall approach to contract negotiation — which involves identifying human rights risks; ensuring that the parties have the mutual capacity to address those risks; budgeting and clearly allocating responsibilities for addressing the risks; and avoiding contractual restraints on the ability to do so — *may offer useful guidance for lawyers in negotiating other contracts that have a potential to impact human rights* (IBA, 2016(a)) (emphasis added).

The ten UNGP Contract Principles help guide the integration of human rights risk management into contract negotiations (HRC, 2011). They include the following elements: ensuring that responsibilities for preventing and mitigating human rights impacts are clarified and agreed before the contract is finalized; provision for transparency; provision for community engagement throughout the lifecycle of the project, and ensuring that the State can monitor the project for compliance with relevant human rights standards whilst also providing the investor with assurance against arbitrary interference. The UNGP Contract Principles also provide for the inclusion of grievance mechanisms for non-contractual harms to third parties. Such mechanisms should ensure that individuals and communities that are impacted by project activities, but are not party to the contract, have access to an effective non-judicial grievance procedure.

Within this general framework, more specific guidance is provided in the VGGT and CFS-RAI, as well as in the OECD/FAO Guidance. As indicated in FAO technical guidance on responsible governance of tenure and the law, lawyers advising companies or investors on business activities that could have a bearing on tenure rights, 'may find the [VGGT] a useful tool …for designing and drafting contracts to mitigate risks associated with gaps or inconsistencies in domestic law and for the undertaking of due diligence' (FAO, 2016(b)).

The CFS-RAI invite contracting parties to consider the UNGP Contract Principles (UNGP 2011(a)) and advise all stakeholders entering into agreements or contracts to adhere to applicable laws and mutually agreed terms and conditions:

> …Contracts should balance the interests of contracting parties, be based on their mutual benefit and be developed in line with the Principles. While negotiating with smallholders, contracting parties are asked to give special consideration to the situation and needs of smallholders.

That special consideration should address the fact that smallholders, and others with customary tenure rights, may not have access to independent legal advice, which may in turn undermine the integrity of the negotiation process. In this regard, FAO technical guidance states:

> …both parties in consultations and negotiations should have legal representation and have access to impact assessments and information identifying all land users, land tenure regimes and land-use patterns (FAO, 2015).

DUE DILIGENCE, TENURE AND AGRICULTURAL INVESTMENT

A guide on the dual responsibilities of private sector lawyers in advising on the acquisition of land and natural resources

Principle 2(iv) of the CFS-RAI highlights the importance, for responsible agricultural investment, of enforceable and fair contracts in generating shared value, thereby contributing to sustainable and inclusive economic development and poverty eradication.

The VGGT and the CFS-RAI, informed by the UNGP Contract Principles, thus set a framework for enforceable and fair contracts with producers and workers which are designed to achieve mutual benefit and safeguard tenure and human rights throughout the lifetime of the investment. A framework which, in line with the general requirements under all those instruments, should be interpreted consistently with international human rights law and ILO standards for labour. These standards could be incorporated by direct reference.

Accordingly, where law firms provide internal precedents for drafting contracts relating to land acquisition, or the purchase of or access to other natural resources for the purposes of agricultural investment, those precedents should be reviewed against the UNGP Contract Principles in order to ensure that they indicate the relevance of the UNGP generally, as well as the VGGT and CFS-RAI in relation to the protection of tenure rights and associated human rights.

> If lawyers are instructed to draft a contract in such a way as to undermine the protection of legitimate tenure rights, or the associated human rights, of those impacted by a project, that instruction should be considered in the light of the UNGP responsibilities to prevent, mitigate, avoid and address adverse impacts on human rights (UNGP 13).

This raises the issue of how lawyers advising investors balance their responsibilities (and those of the client) under the VGGT and CFS-RAI, with their professional duties to the client. If lawyers are instructed to draft a contract in such a way as to undermine the protection of legitimate tenure rights, or the associated human rights, of those impacted by a project, that instruction should be considered in the light of the UNGP responsibilities to prevent, mitigate, avoid and address adverse impacts on human rights (UNGP 13). Lawyers should consider the potential risk that the standards set by the UNGP will be breached. The lawyer should address this risk with the client, consistent with role of 'wise counsellor' as discussed above and exercise leverage to avoid the risk and ensure that both the law firm and the client act in accordance with the UNGP.

This will be relevant to a wide range of contractual issues, including provision for fair levels of compensation where individuals or communities are losing access to land or resources. The human rights impacts of a failure, particularly a deliberate failure, to address the issue of water access again raises a risk of breach of the UNGP direction to avoid and address adverse human rights impacts since the right to an adequate standard of living, the right to food or the right to health of those affected could be prejudiced if access to water is restricted.

As indicated in technical guidance, the impact assessment process should identify who will sign the relevant contracts and, if the government is the formal owner of the land, will have addressed the question as to how users of the land who hold customary or informal use rights will participate in the transaction process and how their rights will be protected under the contract or under side agreements that are enforceable by those users (FAO, 2016).

Technical guidance recommends that the contract should set out a monitoring mechanism, a complaint mechanism and name the court that will be responsible if a case is filed in relation to the investment. To enable the monitoring of contracts and attached provisions, such as environmental and social management plans, the processes related to monitoring, complaint and litigation 'should be communicated widely at local level' (FAO, 2016(a)). Monitoring should specifically address ongoing relationships such as contract farming and outgrowing.

Through their central role in contract negotiation and drafting, lawyers (using their own leverage) may be able to play a critical role in helping a company increase its leverage, as indicated in UNGP 19, in order to encourage or incentivise another party, such as a local investor or replace with a governmental body, to respect human rights (IBA 2016(a)).

UNIDROIT has stated that its future legal guide on agricultural land investment contracts will not endorse large-scale land acquisitions and will raise awareness about alternative investment models. In acknowledging that land acquisitions continue to occur, however, 'the instrument will help to ensure that leases of agricultural land are done responsibly and that stakeholders' rights, including those of legitimate tenure right holders, are both protected and respected' (UNIDROIT, 2018).

The current UNIDROIT outline guide on contract farming addresses a range of issues including: the legal framework, including international human rights treaties; parties, formation and form; obligations and rights of the parties; contractual non-performance; transfer and return; and dispute resolution (UNIDROIT, 2018).[45]

Guidance on the drafting of agricultural investment contracts is also contained in the 2014 IISD Guide to Negotiating Investment Contracts for Farmland and Water (IISD, 2014). The IISD Guide states that it is a legal and policy tool for governments and communities that are involved in negotiating investment contracts with foreign investors. It focuses on a particular type of contract involving long-term leases of farmland.[46] The IISD guide, which refers to the VGGT and CFS-RAI, includes a model contract and provisions addressing tenure and ownership, impacts assessment and a range of other issues.

3.4 TRANSPARENCY, REPORTING AND DISCLOSURE

A lack of transparency in relation to large-scale land transactions has been highlighted (Cotula, 2016). The VGGT make transparency an implementing principle (para. 3B.8) and repeatedly highlight the importance of States and non-State actors ensuring transparency as to land use and tenure rights, providing that all forms of transactions in tenure rights as a result of investments in land, fisheries and forests should be done transparently in line with relevant national sectoral policies. States and other parties are directed to: 'ensure that information on market transactions and information on market values are transparent and widely publicized, subject to privacy restrictions'.

If contracts and impacts assessments are not made public, investors and governmental authorities cannot be held to account for them (Technical Committee, 2014). Investors and those advising them have distinct duties in this regard, concerning their conduct of impact assessment, due diligence and arrangements for monitoring and tracking impacts (FAO, 2016). Technical guidance published by FAO suggests that the following could be made transparent: contracts; ESIAs; feasibility studies, the identity of the ultimate beneficial owner of a project or partner; and 'all other relevant information other than that which is truly confidential from a competitive standpoint' (FAO, 2016).

---

[45] The UNIDROIT/FAO/IFAD Legal Guide on Contract Farming is primarily addressed to the parties to a contract farming relationship and provides advice and guidance on the entire relationship, from negotiation to conclusion, including performance and possible breach or termination of the contract. The Guide provides a description of common contract terms and a discussion of legal issues and critical problems that may arise under various practical situations, illustrating how they may be treated under different legal systems (UNIDROIT, FAO and IFAD, 2015).

[46] Part I of the IISD Guide, Preparing for Negotiations, is designed to assist in the preparatory phase. Part 2, Model Contract, is structured like an investment contract for the lease of farmland and proposes model provisions.

DUE DILIGENCE, TENURE AND AGRICULTURAL INVESTMENT

A guide on the dual responsibilities of private sector lawyers in advising on the acquisition of land and natural resources

Technical guidance on investment safeguards underlines the importance of transparency and disclosure including on contract compliance, impacts and any measures taken or planned to mitigate negative impacts. Investors should also disclose and make publicly available information about the company including its previous experience of similar investments and any 'tenure rights disputes/violations and/or other environmental or social disputes/violations' to which it has been a party. This should continue through the life of the investment (FAO, 2015).

The Reference Annex to the 2016 IBA Guide addresses the issues which may arise for lawyers advising on disclosure and transparency, recognising that lawyers:

> …may be concerned that disclosure of certain information that is critical to the company may then be used against the company in litigation or public campaigns… UNGP 21 recognises that companies cannot be expected to disclose commercially sensitive information, including information that is legally protected against disclosure (IBA, 2016(a)).

The Reference Guide then goes on to point out that: 'At the same time, there may be benefits to the company from increased transparency on human rights that can offset the risks to the company. In the context of tenure rights and associated human rights, lawyers will wish to advise on the specific risks and benefits in each case' (IBA, 2016(a)).

This approach to transparency is likely to exceed the requirements of national law since relatively few States have laws in place which provide for transparency in relation to contract disclosure. Lawyers will advise on the extent to which such an approach is both mandated by international standards and contributes to the prevention and mitigation of human rights impacts by, for example, promoting effective public consultation and planning for mitigation.

UNGP 20 calls on businesses to track the effectiveness of their response to the human rights impacts of their activities in order to verify whether adverse human rights impacts are being addressed. The commentary states that they should make particular efforts to track the effectiveness of their responses to impacts on individuals from groups or populations that may be at heightened risk of vulnerability or marginalization. The Interpretive Guide states that:

> Tracking systems must be credible and robust if they are to help an enterprise know and show that it is respecting human rights. The clearer the indicators and the more comprehensive the processes for gathering information about the enterprise's effectiveness, the better placed it will be to respond to criticism, should it either need or choose to do so (OHCHR, 2012).

Agreements involving large-scale transactions of tenure rights should be monitored, and States should take corrective action to enforce agreements and protect tenure rights where needed (VGGT).[47] This may be particularly relevant to the position of those who have lost forage or grazing rights, those undertaking contract farming or outgrowing arrangements, and those who have been promised benefits to compensate for loss of access to land.

There is growing support for transparency in supply chains which may require transparency in relation to individual commercial agricultural investments (OECD/FAO Guidance).[48] Lawyers should advise on the implications of accounting for human rights impacts through the supply chain from production onwards and as to the risks to the company where these impacts are considered to affect the reputation of products derived from primary production which has infringed tenure rights and associated human rights.

---

[47] See also FAO, 2015, at p. 69.
[48] See Section 2 Model Enterprise Policy for Responsible Agricultural Supply Chains at page 25.

As indicated in technical guidance for investors, there is growing international support for making investment contracts public, including from the UN Special Representative on Business and Human Rights, the IBA and the UN Special Rapporteur on the Right to Food (FAO, 2016). Lawyers will wish to take account of this international support for transparency from leading human rights bodies in the context of advising on transparency and in relation to confidentiality standards where these include a public interest test for disclosure.

Certain businesses will be covered by legal requirements for corporate non-financial reporting on Environmental, Social and Governance reporting (ESG),[49] including as to respect for human rights and their due diligence processes. This should include information relating to tenure rights and associated human rights which falls within these two categories.

3.5 PROTECTION OF ENVIRONMENTAL AND HUMAN RIGHTS DEFENDERS

There is evidence of increasing levels of violence and harassment directed at environmental and land defenders (Cotula and Berger, 2017).[50] The Special Rapporteur on the situation of human rights defenders has stated that the evidence of a threatening environment for defenders is 'oppressive' and worsening in many countries (UNGA, 2015). This includes those involved in issues relating to land and the protection of the environment (UNGA, 2015). The need to address this issue as a human rights risk in the context of large scale land acquisition, and on an ongoing basis, appears evident and is reflected in the VGGT which call on States to respect and protect:

> ...the civil and political rights of defenders of human rights, including the human rights of peasants, indigenous peoples, fishers, pastoralists and rural workers, and should observe their human rights obligations when dealing with individuals and associations acting in defence of land, fisheries and forests.

Technical guidance for investors published by FAO underlines the importance, during the consultation and participation process, of ensuring freedom from retribution and notes that: 'In some settings, individuals may be reluctant to express their opinions in the presence of traditional leaders, government, police or military officials for fear of retribution' (FAO, 2016). For this reason, it may be necessary to hold meetings outside the presence of officials and also to protect community members by having their opinions recorded anonymously.

These concerns are specifically addressed in the recently adopted Escazu Convention.[51] The Escazu Convention, which was negotiated on the basis of the 2012 LAC Declaration on Principle 10,[52] provides at Article 9:

1. Each Party shall guarantee a safe and enabling environment for persons, groups and organizations that promote and defend human rights in environmental matters, so that they are able to act free from threat, restriction and insecurity.

---

[49] As required for certain undertakings under EU Directive 2013/34, as amended by EU Directive 2014/95/EU which places the obligation on 'large undertakings which are public-interest entities exceeding on their balance sheet dates the criterion of the average number of 500 employees during the financial year'. See also the Commission Communication (EU Commission, 2017).

[50] The authors refer to recent research undertaken by Oxfam, Global Witness and the Rights and Resources Initiative.

[51] The Regional Agreement on Access to Information, Public Participation and Justice in Environmental Matters in Latin America and the Caribbean, known as the Escazu Convention, was adopted at Escazu in Costa Rica on 4 March 2018 and opened for signature at the United Nations in September 2018. The Agreement will enter into force on the ninetieth day after the date of deposit of the eleventh instrument of ratification, acceptance, approval or accession, Article 22(1).

[52] Ten Latin American and Caribbean (LAC) countries signed the 2012 Declaration on the application of Principle 10 of the Rio Declaration on Environment and Development in Latin America and the Caribbean ("the LAC Declaration on Principle 10") at Rio+20 in June 2012. Signatories to the Declaration agreed to support the development of a regional instrument which will strengthen access to information, encourage public participation, and strengthen access to justice in sustainable development decision-making.

DUE DILIGENCE, TENURE AND AGRICULTURAL INVESTMENT

A guide on the dual responsibilities of private sector lawyers in advising on the acquisition of land and natural resources

2.   Each Party shall take adequate and effective measures to recognize, protect and promote all the rights of human rights defenders in environmental matters, including their right to life, personal integrity, freedom of opinion and expression, peaceful assembly and association, and free movement, as well as their ability to exercise their access rights, taking into account its international obligations in the field of human rights, its constitutional principles and the basic concepts of its legal system.

3.   Each Party shall also take appropriate, effective and timely measures to prevent, investigate and punish attacks, threats or intimidations that human rights defenders in environmental matters may suffer while exercising the rights set out in the present Agreement.

In the light of the growing risk to defenders, the heightened awareness of the problem and the emerging focus on this issue in international human rights law, lawyers should be vigilant in advising clients on the risks of attacks on those seeking to protect tenure rights and associated rights. These risks relate to the most serious violations of human rights law and rule of law principles and should be a priority for those advising on agricultural investment. Lawyers will wish to consider their own responsibility to avoid and address these human rights violations under the UNGP and in the light of the human rights policy statement adopted by the law firm which should address the issue explicitly, in view of its gravity. Steps to be taken by law firms could include the designation of a partner with specific responsibility for oversight of this issue, specific internal training on the human rights implications of the harassment of defenders as well as dedicated training for clients and the establishment of a rapid response policy in situation where concerns are raised within the firm or by third parties. This issue could be directly addressed in policy statements and engagement letters to signal the seriousness with which the law firm takes the protection of the human rights of defenders, including those protesting against actions of clients of the firm.

3.6   REMEDIATION, GRIEVANCE MECHANISMS AND DISPUTE RESOLUTION

Lawyers and their clients may be faced with a situation where land has been acquired in breach of tenure rights. The requirement, in line with the UNGP, to prevent and mitigate human right impacts and not to cause or contribute to infringements clearly applies in this situation. Technical guidance on FPIC addresses this issue:

> …companies should engage directly with the communities in good faith, explaining the situation. They should then carry out the procedures outlined below and communicate that they will not clear lands or pursue their investment objectives without first recognizing the full extent of customary rights and securing FPIC for their plans from the relevant rights-holders (FAO, 2014).

It does need to be recognized, however, that such situations place affected communities in a position of considerable disadvantage. Once their lands have been allocated to a third party without their consent, the leverage of communities in any subsequent negotiations with the company is substantially weakened (FAO, 2014).

This technical guidance addresses the specific situation of indigenous peoples and their right to FPIC.[53] However similar issues will affect other communities whose tenure rights have been infringed in this way. A critical factor in this situation, and more generally, is that local communities are unlikely to have access to legal and technical advice during the consultation

---

[53] See also CFS-RAI Principle 9, para. 29(iv), FAO, 2014, p.17.

process. Lawyers should be aware of potential conflicts of interest if their client pays for such advice and that steps should be taken to mitigate the situation by seeking to ensure that communities have access to genuinely independent advice and support.

As part of their responsibility to respect human rights, businesses must have in place processes to enable the remediation of any adverse human rights impacts they cause or to which they have contributed (UNGP 15(c)). UNGP 22 states that:

> Where business enterprises identify that they have caused or contributed to adverse impacts, they should provide for or cooperate in their remediation through legitimate processes.

Law firms will need to advise clients on processes for remediation, as well as considering processes of their own in cases where they may have contributed to adverse impacts. As stated above, firms will wish to take proactive steps to avoid contributing to (and it goes without saying, causing), or being linked to, adverse impacts on human rights so far as is consistent with professional obligations and bearing in mind whether they should withdraw services in certain cases (see Section 2.2).

The VGGT implementing principles include accountability and the VGGT confirm that businesses should provide operational level grievance mechanisms where appropriate, where they have caused or contributed to adverse impacts (VGGT), thus incorporating the duties laid down in the UNGP.[54] VGGT 21 sets out the duties of states to provide access to 'timely, affordable and effective means of resolving disputes over tenure rights, including alternative means of resolving such disputes'.

> VGGT 21 sets out the duties of states to provide access to 'timely, affordable and effective means of resolving disputes over tenure rights, including alternative means of resolving such disputes'.

Law firms can play a key role in ensuring that grievance mechanisms meet standards of fairness and due process, including by ensuring that communities are independently and legally represented in accordance with their own wishes. As recognised by the IBA, the UNGPs were not intended to override or supplement legal professional codes of conduct, given the critical role that lawyers play in upholding the rule of law and supporting the administration of justice.[55] That critical role allows lawyers, whilst upholding their clients best interests and given their particular expertise, to advise on processes that reduce the risk of the client being found to have undermined the rule of law, by ensuring that grievance mechanisms meet standards of due process.

Lawyers can also advise on the design of processes that are tailored to the cultural and specific approaches of the community or stakeholders concerned, for example by ensuring that interpretation is available where necessary, that time-frames accord with the community's own processes for internal decision-making and that, overall, a level playing field is applied in accordance with access to justice principles. Lawyers should bear in mind the OECD/FAO direction that businesses should:

> Avoid using grievance mechanisms established by enterprises to preclude access to judicial or non-judicial grievance mechanisms, including the [National Contact Points] under the OECD Guidelines, or to undermine the role of trade unions in addressing labour-related disputes (OECD/FAO Guidance).

As the IBA has reiterated in its recent guidance, business clients are entitled to mount a defence to allegations that they have breached tenure rights or associated human rights and their legal

---

[54] See also CFS-RAI Principle 9 (FAO, 2014, p.17 and FAO, 2015, pp.72-74); FAO, 2016(b), p.87 et seq. and FAO, 2016 at p.39 et seq.
[55] IBA, 2016, pp. 27-28.

DUE DILIGENCE, TENURE AND AGRICULTURAL INVESTMENT

A guide on the dual responsibilities of private sector lawyers in advising on the acquisition of land and natural resources

advisors can represent them for these purposes. In advising and representing clients however, the standards underpinning the UNGP, including due diligence, should be reflected in advice and other support offered by law firms and internal counsel consistent with the standards set by professional bodies, including the IBA. In the specific case of large scale land acquisitions for agriculture and related investments, those standards should be informed by the VGGT, the CFS-RAI and the OECD/FAO Guidance and related technical guidance, as well as international human rights laws and jurisprudence.

CONCLUSIONS

4. CONCLUSIONS

The VGGT, together with CFS-RAI, represent an international response to the serious risks posed to tenure rights, and associated human rights, by weak governance of tenure. That response reflects, and is informed by, international human rights law. Breach of the standards laid down in those instruments poses a risk to the fulfilment of a range of human rights obligations including the right to life, the right to health and the right to food, as well as civil and political rights. The ways in which human rights law is relevant to, and addresses, the impacts of large scale agricultural investments are extensively covered in FAO's technical guidance, and in human rights jurisprudence and the reports of human rights bodies, as well as in the writings of commentators. The CFS-RAI and OECD/FAO Guidance support the standards laid down in the VGGT and provide further guidance in observing other relevant human rights.

Within that legal and policy framework, lawyers advise and assist corporate clients involved in agricultural investments, in accordance with professional standards and in the light of their dual responsibilities under the UNGP, as advisors to businesses and as businesses in their own right. The IBA has addressed the implications of the UNGP for law firms and for the independent responsibilities of lawyers as have some regional and national professional bodies.

Taking into account the evolving practice in seeking to integrate UNGP standards with professional rules, and in the context of large-scale agricultural investment in countries where tenure governance is weak, or subject to ongoing reform, the following recommendations are suggested:

- Law firms should review their internal policies on human rights and on the implementation of the UNGP in order to ensure that these incorporate explicit consideration of the protection of legitimate tenure rights as this impacts, or may impact, on compliance with associated human rights. The overall aim should be to prevent, mitigate, avoid and address adverse impacts on human rights both on behalf of the client, and on behalf of the firm as a business in its own right. The review should refer to and be informed by the VGGT, the CFS-RAI and the OECD/ FAO Guidance and associated technical guidance. This includes a review of relevant policy statements, engagement letters, internal training and capacity building, as well as the conduct of due diligence;

- In order to facilitate the review suggested above, by promoting a broader and deeper engagement with the UNGP and specifically with tenure and associated human rights, law firms may wish to ensure that all relevant departments take joint responsibility for UNGP implementation, where this is not already the case. To ensure that all relevant areas of work are covered in relation to the protection of tenure rights and associated human rights, it may be appropriate for each department of the firm to adhere to a specific policy in this area and to review resources and expertise to ensure effective coverage;

- In-house lawyers should review the company's operating policies, precedents and training materials. The review should explicitly refer to and be informed by the VGGT, the CFS-RAI and the OECD/FAO Guidance and associated technical guidance, together with the UNGP. They should ensure that the company has a policy on due diligence which enables it to meet international standards on the protection of tenure rights in the area of agricultural investment, and in particular, to avoid and address adverse human rights impacts;

DUE DILIGENCE, TENURE AND AGRICULTURAL INVESTMENT

A guide on the dual responsibilities of private sector lawyers in advising on the acquisition of land and natural resources

- Law firms should ensure that they advise clients on the implications of the VGGT, CFS-RAI and OECD/FAO Guidance as internationally accepted good practice in the context of agricultural investment. These standards should be considered when advising on large-scale acquisition of land and other natural resources, including in the context of due diligence. Legal advisors should ensure that all legal, reputational and financial risks associated with breach of these international standards are brought to the attention of clients, including in the context of due diligence;

- Assessment of legal risk is a particular area where engagement with the UNGP generally, and with the protection of tenure rights and associated human rights in particular, can be addressed effectively. This is an area where the concepts of the role of the 'wise counsellor' and leverage, as highlighted recently by the IBA, are particularly relevant. Firms may wish to review, on an ongoing basis, the extent to which these concepts facilitate the resolution of operational issues relating to advice and other work relating to large-scale land acquisitions. Dialogue with existing or new clients concerning these issues may be helpful in advance of specific issues arising;

- Firms should give specific guidance on due diligence so that negative human rights impacts can be prevented, mitigated, avoided and addressed by the client, taking into account the technical guidance available in relation to agricultural investment, as well as the general guidance issued in association with the UNGP and by the OHCHR, the IBA and others;

- In relation to the drafting of contracts, lawyers should advise that the key issues should be addressed in line with standards laid down in the VGGT and associated human rights, including early meaningful consultation and participation of those likely to be impacted by the investment, transparency, remediation and grievance procedures. Contracts should provide for the prevention of or mitigation of impacts. This can be achieved through the provision of specific benefits and commitments; provision for transparency as to the investor and the investment; the protection of user rights and access to water; the inclusion of explicit monitoring and reporting arrangements and the incorporation of appropriate dispute or grievance mechanisms;

- Law firms should be vigilant to the need to advise clients on the importance of promoting the protection of environmental and human rights defenders who are involved in actions relating to the client's investments. The firm should have a clear policy on addressing this issue operationally in a swift and effective way having regard to the protection of fundamental human rights; and

- Firms should endeavour to ensure that grievance processes are designed and conducted in accordance with due process and fairness standards, and that any tension between these and their professional duty to the client should be raised with the client. The firm should act as a 'wise counsellor' and use its leverage with the client to promote fair and independent adjudications on disputes.

There is a clear opportunity for law firms which have taken effective measures to address the firm's responsibilities under the UNGP and have sought to implement the standards of the VGGT and CFS-RAI in their work, and on behalf of their clients, to demonstrate best practice in this area. Through requirements for non-financial reporting and other means, firms can showcase their approach as representing best practice in the legal sector. In taking meaningful steps to integrate these standards into the work of the firm, firms will be better placed to assure clients that they are supported in a comprehensive and practical way to comply with these international standards, to minimise the reputational, legal, financial and other risks associated with non-compliance and the risk of disputes and actions which cause grave damage to rights of the communities affected and pose risks to the success, inclusiveness and sustainability, of investments undertaken by the client.

REFERENCES

CASES

Centre for Minority Rights Development (Kenya) and Minority Rights Group International on behalf of Endorois Welfare Council v. Kenya, 4 February 2010. African Commission for Human and People's Rights (ACHPR), 276.2003.

Kichwa Indigenous People of Sarayaku v. Ecuador. 27 June 2012. Inter-American Court of Human Rights (IACtHR).

Saramaka People v Suriname. 28 November 2007. IACtHR.

Sawhoyamaxa Indigenous Community v. Paraguay. 29 March 2006. IACtHR.

Yakye Axa Indigenous Community v. Paraguay. June 17 2005. IACtHR.

INTERNATIONAL INSTRUMENTS

Legally-binding

International Covenant on Civil and Political Rights (ICCPR). 1966. Adopted by UNGA Resolution 2200A (XXI) on 16 December 1966 and in force from 23 March 1976.

International Covenant of Economic, Social and Cultural Rights (ICESCR). 1966. Adopted by UNGA Resolution 2200A (XXI) on 16 December 1966 and in force from 3 January 1976.

OECD Convention on Combating Bribery of Foreign Public Officials in International Business Transactions. Adopted by the Negotiating Conference on 21 November 1997 and in force from 15 February 1999.

Regional Agreement on Access to Information, Participation and Justice in Environmental Matters in Latin America and the Caribbean. 2018. Adopted at Escazú, Costa Rica, on 4 March 2018. Open for signature at United Nations Headquarters in New York on 27 September 2018 (not yet in force). Costa Rica.

UN Convention against Corruption (UNCAC). 2003. Adopted by UNGA Rresolution 58/4 on 31 October 2003 and in force from 14 December 2005.

Non-legally-binding

African Union, African Development Bank and United Nations Economic Commission for Africa. 2014. *Guiding Principles on Large Scale Land Based Investments in Africa.* Addis Ababa. 42 pp.

Committee on World Food Security (CFS). 2012. *Voluntary Guidelines on the Responsible Governance of Tenure of Land, Fisheries and Forests in the Context of National Food Security.* Committee on World Food Security, May 2012. Rome.

DUE DILIGENCE, TENURE AND AGRICULTURAL INVESTMENT

A guide on the dual responsibilities of private sector lawyers in advising on the acquisition of land and natural resources

CFS. 2014. *Principles for the Responsible Investment in Agriculture and Food Systems (CFS-RAI) endorsed by the Committee on World Food Security.* Rome.

European Commission. 2017. *Guidelines on non-financial reporting (methodology for reporting non-financial information).*

FAO. 2004. *Voluntary Guidelines to support the progressive realization of the right to adequate food in the context of national food security.* Committee on World Food Security and FAO Council. Rome.

FAO. 2015. *Voluntary Guidelines for Securing Sustainable Small-Scale Fisheries in the Context of Food Security and Poverty Eradication.* Adopted by the FAO Committee on Fisheries. Rome.

Human Rights Council. 2011. *Guiding Principles on Business and Human Rights: Implementing the United Nations 'Protect, Respect and Remedy' Framework.* Endorsed by resolution 17/4 of the UN Human Rights Council, entitled Human Rights and Transnational Corporations and Other Business Enterprises, A/HRC/RES/17/4. New York and Geneva.

OECD. *Guidelines for Multinational Enterprises.* 2011.

OECD-FAO. 2016. *OECD-FAO Guidance for Responsible Agricultural Supply Chains.* OECD Publishing. Paris. [also available at http://dx.doi.org/10.1787/9789264251052-en]

United Nations. 2007. *United Nations Declaration on the Rights of Indigenous Peoples.* Resolution adopted by the General Assembly on 13 September 2007. New York.

United Nations. 2015. *Transforming our world: the 2030 Agenda for Sustainable Development.* Resolution adopted by the General Assembly on 25 September 2015.

LITERATURE

American Bar Association (ABA). 2016. *American Bar Association Model Rules 2016.* [also available at www.americanbar.org/groups/professional_responsibility/publications/model_rules_of_professional_conduct/rule_2_1_advisor.html].

ActionAid. 2015. *New Alliance New Risk of Land Grabs Evidence from Malawi, Nigeria, Senegal and Tanzania.*

Council of Bars and Law Societies of Europe (CBBE). 2017. *Practical Issues for Bars and Law Societies on Corporate Social Responsibility Guidance III.* Brussels. [also available at www.ccbe.eu].

Committee on the Elimination of All Forms of Discrimination Against Women (CEDAW). 2016. *General Recommendation No. 34 on the Rights of Rural Women.* CEDAW/C/GC/34.

Committee on Economic, Social and Cultural Rigts (CESCR). 1997. *CESCR General Comment No. 7: The Right to adequate housing: forced evictions.*

Cotula, L. 2016. 'Land Grabbing' and International Investment Law: Towards a Global Reconfiguration of Property. *Yearbook on International Investment Law & Policy 2014-2015.* Oxford University Press.

Cotula, L., Berger, T. 2017. *Trends in global land use investment: implications for legal empowerment.* IIED.

Cotula, L. 2017(a). International Soft-law Instruments and Global Resource Governance: Reflections on the Voluntary Guidelines on the Responsible Governance of Tenure. 13/2 *Law, Environment and Development Journal*, 115 pp. [also available at http://www.lead-journal.org/content/17115.pdf].

Cotula, L. 2017(b). Land, property and sovereignty in international law. *Cardozo Journal of International and Comparative Law.*Vol 25, pp. 219-286.

FAO. 2013. *Governing land for women and men: A technical guide to support the achievement of responsible gender-equitable governance of land tenure.* Governance of tenure technical guide No. 1. Rome.

FAO. 2014. *Respecting free, prior and informed consent: Practical guidance for governments, companies, NGOs, indigenous peoples and local communities in relation to land acquisition.* Governance of Tenure Technical Guide No. 3. Rome.

FAO. 2015. *Safeguarding land tenure rights in the context of agricultural investment.* Governance of Tenure Technical Guide No. 4. Rome.

FAO. 2016. *Responsible governance of tenure: a technical guide for investors.* Governance of Tenure Technical Guide No. 7. Rome.

FAO. 2016(a). *Governing tenure rights to commons.* Governance of Tenure Technical Guide No 8. Rome.

FAO. 2016(b). *Responsible governance of tenure and the law: A guide for lawyers and other legal service providers.* Governance of Tenure Technical Guide No. 5. Rome.

FAO. 2016(c). *Assessment of international labour standards that apply to rural employment: An overview for the work of FAO relating to labour protection in agriculture, forestry and fisheries.* FAO Legal Papers No 100. Rome.

FAO. 2018. *Realizing women's rights to land in the law: A guide for reporting on SDG indicator 5.a.2.* Rome.

Human Rights Council (HRC). 2007. *Basic principles and guidelines on development-based evictions and displacement*, Annex 1 of the report of the Special Rapporteur on adequate housing as a component of the right to an adequate standard of living, A/HRC/4/18. New York and Geneva. [also available at http://www.ohchr.org/Documents/Issues/Housing/Guidelines_en.pdf].

HRC. 2009. *Large-scale land acquisitions and leases: A set of minimum principles and measures to address the human rights challenge.* A/HRC/13/33/Add.2.

HRC. 2011. *Report of the Special Representative of the Secretary General on the issue of human rights and transnational corporations and other business enterprises, John Ruggie Addendum: Principles for responsible contracts: integrating the management of human rights risks into State-investor contract negotiations: guidance for negotiators.* A/HRC/17/31/Add. 3.

A guide on the dual responsibilities of private sector lawyers in advising on the acquisition of land and natural resources

HRC. 2012. *Report by the Special Rapporteur on the situation of human rights in Cambodia: A human rights analysis of economic and other land concessions in Cambodia.* A/HRC/ 21/ 63/ Add.1.

General Assembly (GA). 2012. *The right to food. Interim report of the Special Rapporteur on the right to food, Mr Oivier de Schutter.* A/67/268.

GA. 2012(a). Final study of the Human Rights Council Advisory Committee on the advancement of the rights of peasants and other people working in rural areas. A/HRC/19/75.

GA. 2015. Situation of human rights defenders. Report of the Special Rapporteur on the situation of human rights defenders, Mr. Michel Forst. A/HRC/28/63.

International Bar Association (IBA). 2011. International Principles on Conduct for the Legal Profession (IBA International Principles).

IBA. 2015. Business and Human Rights Guidance for Bar Associations (IBA Bar Association Guide).

IBA. 2016. Practical Guide for Business Lawyers on Business and Human Rights (IBA Practical Guide).

IBA 2016(a). *Reference Annex to the IBA Practical Guide on Business and Human Rights for Business Lawyers.*

International Finance Corporation (IFC). 2012. *IFC Performance Standards on Environmental and Social Sustainability.*

International Institute for Sustainable Development (IISD). 2014. *The IISD Guide to Negotiating Investment Contracts for Farmland and Water: Part II Model Contract.*

Internal Land Coalition (ILC). 2011. *Securing land access for the poor in times of intensified natural resources competition.* The Tirana Declaration was endorsed by the ILC Assembly of Members on 27 May 2011.

Law Society of England and Wales. 2016. *Business and human rights: a practical guide.* The Law Society of England and Wales. London.

Law Firm Business and Human Rights Peer Learning Process. 2016. *Emerging Practice, Insights and Reflections - Workshop Report.* [also available at https://www.business-humanrights.org/ sites/default/files/documents/Law%20Firm%20BHR%20Peer%20Learning%20Process%20 Report%20-%20FINAL%20ONLINE.pdf].

Luban, D., Wendel, B. 2017. *Philosophical Legal Ethics: An Affectionate History.* The Georgetown Journal of Legal Ethics [Vol 30: 337 2017].

OHCHR. 2012. *The Corporate Responsibility to Respect Human Rights* (Interpretive Guide) HR/ PUB/12/02. United Nations.

Oxfam. 2011. *Land and Power: The Growing Scandal Surrounding the New Wave of Investments in Land.* Oxfam Briefing Paper, 15–16, [also available at http:// www.oxfam.org/ sites/ www. oxfam.org/ files/ file_ attachments/ bp151- land- power- rights- acquisitions- 220911- en 4.pdf]

Pepper, S.L. 2015. *Three Dichotomies in Lawyers' Ethics (With Particular Attention to the Corporation as Client).* Georgetown Journal of Legal Ethics, Vol. 28, No. 4.

Ruggie, J.G. 2017. *The Social Construction of the UN Guiding Principles on Business and Human Rights.* Corporate Responsibility Initiative Working Paper No. 67. Cambridge, MA: John F. Kennedy School of Government, Harvard University.

Sherman, J.F. 2013. *The UN Guiding Principles: Practical Implications for Business Lawyers.* In-House Defense Quarterly Winter 2013.

Technical Committee. 2014. *Technical Committee on Land and Development Guide to due diligence of agribusiness projects that affect land and property rights, Operational guide.* France. [also available at http://www.landcoalition.org/sites/default/files/documents/resources/Guide-to-due-diligence.pdf].

International Institute for the Unification of Private Law (UNIDROIT). 2018. *Private Law and agricultural development: An overview of UNIDROIT's work on agricultural land investment contracts. Preparing, negotiating and implementing an agricultural land investment contract that is consistent with the VGGT and CFS-RAI Principles.* [also available at https://www.unidroit.org/english/documents/2018/study80b/s-80b-overview-e.pdf].

UNIDROIT/FAO/IFAD. 2015. *Legal Guide on Contract Farming.* Rome.

Windfuhr, M. 2017. *Safeguarding Human Rights in Land-Related Investments: Comparison of the Voluntary Guidelines on Land with the IFC Performance Standards and the World BankEnvironmental and Social Safeguard Framework.* German Institute for Human Rights. [also available at http://www.institutfuer-menschenrechte.de/fileadmin/user_upload/Publikationen/ANALYSE/Analyse__Safeguarding_Human_Rights_in_Land_Related_Investments_bf.pdf].